We are now forn ~~government.~~ *government.*
Real liberty is neither found in despotism,
nor in the extremes of democracy,
but in moderate governments.

ALEXANDER HAMILTON
at the Constitutional Convention

ANGRY MOBS AND FOUNDING FATHERS

THE FIGHT FOR CONTROL OF THE AMERICAN REVOLUTION

MICHAEL E. NEWTON

Eleftheria Publishing

Published by Eleftheria Publishing
www.eleftheriapublishing.com

ISBN-10: 0-9826040-2-5
ISBN-13: 978-0-9826040-2-1
Library of Congress Control Number: 2011-930267

Printed in the United States of America

CONTENTS

PREFACE

The American Revolution began as a grass-roots rebellion against British oppression. Thousands of colonists protested, petitioned Parliament, boycotted British merchants and goods, harassed British officials, overthrew colonial governments, and waged open war against the British army.

In the desire to tell a good story, historians have searched for the leaders of this rebellion—men such as Samuel Adams and Patrick Henry. But this rebellion had no leaders and no organizers. Instead, rebellions sprang up throughout the colonies in response to acts of British oppression.

Not everyone fully agreed with these angry mobs. Those who had studied political philosophy and history feared this democratic and anarchic rebellion. These men dreaded the destruction the British army would inflict and worried that America could lose this war against Britain. More so, they worried that "the multitude, the vulgar, the herd, the rabble, the mob"[1] were destroying law and order. They feared that the colonists would fail to establish a government capable of protecting the life, liberty, and property of all Americans if they were to win independence.

Five years after declaring independence, eight years after the Boston Tea Party, eleven years after the Boston Massacre, and more than fifteen years after the first protests against the Sugar and Stamp Acts, the American army defeated General Cornwallis's army of 9,000 troops in the Battle of Yorktown. Two years later, the Treaty of Paris officially granted America its independence. The war was over, America had its independence, but the revolution continued.

To overthrow a government is common in history. To establish a stable republican government out of chaos and anarchy is unique. After the war, the thirteen sovereign states coexisted under the Articles of Confederation, but the Confederation government was powerless and ineffective. "After an unequivocal experience of the inefficacy of the subsisting federal government,"[2] Congress called for a convention of the country's greatest minds to revise the Articles of Confederation. Instead, the Founding Fathers created the Constitution, a document even more revolutionary than the war America had just won.

The battle between liberty and power continued in the new republic, as it has throughout history. Today, more than 200 years later, the United States is still trying to "improve and perpetuate"[3] the government it inherited from the angry mobs, who started the American Revolution, and the Founding Fathers, who created this great republic.

CHAPTER ONE

ANGRY MOBS
IN COLONIAL AMERICA

In the mid-1700s, colonial America experienced record-breaking growth. Immigrants flooded into the colonies, rates of marriage and childbirth were high, and the economy expanded with the rising population. No central government existed and the small state governments were primarily concerned with defense against foreigners and Indians. Most societal affairs were managed at the town level, each being its own democracy. Taxes were virtually nonexistent and white Americans were among the wealthiest people on earth.

Yet the colonists became increasingly dissatisfied with colonial rule as Britain took a more active role in American affairs. The British limited westward expansion, instituted new taxes, enacted new mercantilist laws, and infringed on American self-rule. At first, the colonists lodged complaints and petitioned the British government. Then they peacefully protested and boycotted British goods. Finally, their previous demonstrations going unheeded, they rebelled against British tyranny and declared their independence.

COLONIAL AMERICANS

The thirteen colonies belonged to the British Empire and its residents were British subjects, but most colonists were not of British descent. Thomas Paine explained in *Common Sense*, "Europe, and not England, is the parent country of America."[1] Paine added, "Not one third of the inhabitants, even of this province, are of English descent."[2] Instead, America was a mix of British, Irish, Scottish, Scots-Irish, Dutch, French, German, African, and other nationalities. Initially, nearly 90 percent of European immigrants into the thirteen colonies were British. However, after 1680, only a quarter of European immigrants were British.[3] More important, because of the high birth rate, most colonists were born in America. Consequently, by the latter half of the 1700s, the colonists discarded their ancestral heritage and began referring to themselves as Americans.[4]

The first United States census conducted in 1790 found that 61 percent of whites were of British descent.[5] Adding in the black population, those of British descent were just under half of the total population. However, this number represents the upper limit for British-Americans. Those with mixed ancestry likely claimed British heritage to fit in better. Similarly, many foreigners anglicized their names to assimilate more easily into the Anglo-American culture. For example, a French Huguenot named Apollos Rivoire became Paul Revere, father of the more famous Paul Revere of the American Revolution.

Although colonists of British descent composed one-third to one-half of the total population, they were not equally distributed throughout the colonies. Massachusetts was the most British with about 85 percent of its population descending from British immigrants, according to one estimate. In Connecticut, the figure was about 75 percent. It was approximately 65 percent in Rhode Island, 45 percent in New York, Maryland, and North Carolina, 40 percent in New Jersey, 35 percent in Virginia, and 30 percent in Pennsylvania.[6]

Massachusetts, with the highest proportion of people of British descent, ignited the first sparks of rebellion, whereas some of the most Loyalist areas—New York, New Jersey, and Pennsylvania—were among the most non-British. The areas with larger proportions of colonists of British descent had numerous reasons to favor independence. When Britain attacked their rights as British citizens, they were the first to defend those rights, just as the British people had done for many centuries. In contrast, the immigrants arriving from the rest of Europe knew they would be in the minority, expected to live under the rules of others, and were not as upset by their lack of power within the political system. Furthermore, those of British descent, having immigrated to America earlier than others, felt greater loyalty to their adopted country and were quicker to defend it against wrongs committed by Britain.

In reality, though, a large percentage of the Britons who immigrated to America were not considered upstanding citizens back in Britain. Many immigrated to America to escape poverty. Britain's highly structured society made it incredibly difficult for a poor person to climb the economic ladder. In America, these poor people had a chance to succeed and many did.

Britain also sent many criminals to America. Nearly a quarter of all British immigrants arriving in the colonies were convicts shipped off by the British government.[7] Not only did these felons have no allegiance to Britain, but the residents of the American colonies resented Britain for sending them over. In 1751, Benjamin Franklin likened these British "felons-convict" to rattlesnakes and humorously proposed that, in exchange for the convicts that Britain sends to America, "some thousands" of rattlesnakes "might be collected annually and transported to Britain. There I would propose to have them carefully distributed in St. James Park." Franklin concluded that "as in every other branch of trade," Britain "will have the advantage" over America because "the rattle-snake gives warning before he attempts his mischief; which the convict does not."[8]

Furthermore, many immigrants to the colonies, most notably the Puritans, fled civil and religious persecution in Britain and Europe. Thomas Paine remarked, "This new world hath been the asylum for the persecuted lovers of civil and religious liberty from every part of Europe. Hither have they fled, not from the tender embraces of the mother, but from the cruelty of the monster; and it is so far true of England, that the same tyranny which drove the first emigrants from home, pursues their descendants still."[9]

In total, Britain's American colonies were not very British. Fully, one-half to two-thirds of the colonists were not of British descent. A quarter of the British immigrants were convicts. Many immigrants had left their mother countries because of religious persecution or economic hardship. And with nearly half of the American population at the time of the revolution under the age of sixteen, all memory of the friendly relationship between America and Britain was quickly lost when British oppression began.[10] As a result, loyalty to Britain was low and the colonists increasingly saw themselves as Americans instead of British subjects.

NO TAXATION WITHOUT REPRESENTATION

Taxes in colonial America were virtually nonexistent. In 1765, colonists in British America paid taxes of just two to four percent of what British citizens paid back in England.[11] Historian Paul Johnson writes:

> The American mainland colonies were the least taxed territories on earth. Indeed, it is probably true to say that colonial America was the least taxed country in recorded history. Government was extremely small, limited in its powers, and cheap.[12]

A large and populous country cannot be administered and defended without cost. Taxes were too low to cover expenses, especially after Britain's financial condition deteriorated during the Seven Years War with France, much of which was fought in North America as the French and Indian War.[13] Prior to the Seven Years War, Britain had debts of £72 million. The war doubled that to £140 million.[14] Adam Smith explains, "That public debt has been contracted in the defence, not of Great Britain alone, but of all the different provinces of the empire; the immense debt contracted in the late war in particular, and a great part of that contracted in the war before, were both properly contracted in defence of America."[15]

Annual interest of £5 million consumed about sixty percent of the British government's budget.[16] Spending cuts alone could not balance the budget, so Britain sought increased tax revenue. With the average American paying just a shilling a year in taxes,[17] Britain expected the colonists to pay more.

On top of that, the cost of defending America increased after Britain won new territories during the French and Indian War. To control this larger territory, defend it from Indian attack, and to quell any French rebellions in the newly captured Canada, Britain increased the size of its standing army in North America from 3,100 to 7,500 troops.[18]

Americans not only refused to pay for these troops, but they also saw this army as a threat to their liberty. The Declaration of Independence complained that Britain "kept among us, in times of peace, standing armies without the consent of our legislature." Furthermore, the Americans argued that France attacked the colonies during the French and Indian War, not because they were Americans, but because they were British. Thomas Paine wrote in *Common Sense*, "France and Spain never were, nor perhaps ever will be our enemies as Americans, but as our being the subjects of Great-Britain."[19] Because the French and Indian War was a British war, not an American one, the colonists argued that Britain should bear the expense of that war. Additionally, the colonists pointed out that with the French out of North America and the Spanish far off to the west on the other side of the Mississippi River, the colonies needed less defense after the French and Indian War, not more.

Most of all, Americans asked why they should pay taxes as British citizens if they did not have representation like those living in Britain. They cried "no taxation without representation" to little avail. Britain needed money to pay the interest on its debt and to defend its American territories. If the colonies would not pay voluntarily, Britain would try to take the money forcibly.

The Sugar Act of 1764 imposed a tax on sugar to help pay for the defense of America and repay the debt incurred fighting the French and Indian War. America boycotted British imports in protest and smuggled in sugar to avoid the tax. Britain quickly repealed the tax, primarily because the cost to administer it was four times greater than the revenue collected.[20] Americans noted how their protests, boycotts, and smuggling successfully overturned Britain's attempt to tax them. They would use these strategies again and again to resist British intrusions into colonial affairs, until more forceful tactics proved necessary.

Britain again tried to raise taxes on its American colonies, but the Stamp Act of 1765 was an even bigger failure than the Sugar Act and was a primary cause of the initial rebellion and subsequent revolution against British rule. The Stamp Act enacted a tax on most papers and printed materials. Everything from legal documents, magazines, and newspapers to dice and playing cards needed a stamp verifying the tax was paid. Furthermore, the tax had to be paid in British currency, which was in short supply in the colonies because of British monetary and mercantilist policies.

The tax rates established by the Stamp Act were not particularly onerous, but for many colonists it was the first tax they ever paid.[21] Previously, taxes had been indirectly applied, primarily in the form of tariffs, and most Americans barely knew they were there. However, the Stamp Tax was directly felt, seen, and paid by almost all Americans. Furthermore, this bothersome tax required the people to pay a tax and receive a stamp on each and every document. The taxes paid were secondary to the harassment the people suffered from the new tax collectors. The Declaration of Independence complained that Britain "has erected a multitude of New Offices, and sent hither swarms of Officers to harass our people and eat out their substance."

The colonists resisted this direct and bothersome tax. Newspapers vilified the British government. Colonial governments formally declared their dissatisfaction. Rhode Island declared the Stamp Act "unconstitutional." Patrick Henry introduced resolutions in the Virginia House of Burgesses asserting that only their elected representatives had the right to tax them. The Virginia House of Burgesses passed these resolutions, but Henry also introduced more extreme resolutions that they deemed too treasonous. Nevertheless, the newspapers printed all of Henry's resolutions as the people of Virginia asserted their independence, in spirit if not in law.[22] Nine colonies sent representatives to the Stamp Act Congress that produced a Declaration of Rights and Grievances, stating:

> That it is inseparably essential to the freedom of a people, and the undoubted rights of Englishmen, that no taxes should be imposed on them, but with their own consent, given personally, or by their representatives...

> That the duties imposed by several late acts of Parliament, from the peculiar circumstances of these colonies, will be extremely burthensome and grievous, and, from the scarcity of specie, the payment of them absolutely impracticable...

> That the increase, prosperity, and happiness of these colonies depend on the full and free enjoyment of their rights

and liberties, and an intercourse, with Great Britain, mutually affectionate and advantageous…

That it is the indispensable duty of these colonies…to procure the repeal of the act for granting and applying certain stamp duties…[23]

When the colonies sent their petitions to Britain, Parliament refused to even consider them. It was bad enough that Parliament had passed a bill so unpopular in America, but it was even worse that they totally ignored the colonists' grievances. The colonists thought that an ally would at least listen and consider their claims. By ignoring them, the colonists thought that Britain was acting like a tyrant. As Jefferson wrote in the Declaration of Independence: "In every stage of these Oppressions We have Petitioned for Redress in the most humble terms: Our repeated Petitions have been answered only by repeated injury. A Prince, whose character is thus marked by every act which may define a Tyrant, is unfit to be the ruler of a free people."

When the colonies exhausted their official means of protest, they used alternative methods of demonstrating their disapproval.[24] American merchants issued calls for the boycott of British goods. The boycott succeeded. British exports to the colonies fell by nearly two thirds. Unemployment in Britain rose. British workers rioted. British merchants and industrialists petitioned Parliament to repeal the Stamp Act.[25]

Riots began in Massachusetts and spread throughout the thirteen colonies. Stamp agents were threatened and forced to quit. The colonists burned effigies of royal officials as they proclaimed "Liberty, Property, and No Stamps." They attacked and ransacked houses belonging to tax collectors and other government officials. An angry mob even attacked the house of Benjamin Franklin, Pennsylvania's representative to the British Parliament, because he was incorrectly but understandably seen as a supporter of the Stamp Act, especially after he recommended his friend for the post of tax collector.[26] Parliament repealed the Stamp Act just one year after they passed it and less than five months after it had gone into effect.

In *The American Revolution: A History*, Gordon Wood writes, "ultimately it was mob violence that destroyed the Stamp Act in America."[27] The angry mobs had exerted their power and won. Angry mobs were more powerful than kings or parliaments. The colonists learned that each time Britain imposed or raised taxes, they could resist with boycotts, with pamphlets and newspapers defending American liberties and attacking British tyranny, and even with violence and lawlessness if necessary. The colonists had found their means of resisting British oppression.

The purpose of the stamp tax was to cover the expense of British troops stationed in America. However, because the boycotts led to a sharp decline in tariff revenue, Britain could no longer afford to defend the American frontier. To save money, Britain withdrew many of its troops from the West and closed a number of outposts.[28] Even though many colonists desired this, it led to increased lawlessness in the West and diminished respect for British rule among Americans.

The Stamp Act united the colonies for the first time. In most respects, colonists in New England had few similarities with those in the South except for language. But a common enemy unites people and the colonists began defining themselves not as British subjects or as residents of their individual colonies, but as Americans. The Stamp Act Congress that sent its formal protest to the British government in London was the first independent gathering of the colonies.[29] Britain saw this increasing unity among the colonies as a threat to its control over them.

While the boycotts had the desired effect of harming the British economy, it also contributed to a severe economic downturn in America. Tobacco prices fell by 75 percent, businesses failed, and the number of personal bankruptcies increased. The colonists blamed Britain for the depression.[30] Furthermore, the Stamp Act angered some of the most important and influential groups in the colonies, including merchants, lawyers, and publishers.[31] The trade dispute with Britain encouraged America to accelerate its industrialization, making Americans even less reliant on Britain.

The resentment did not disappear after Britain repealed the Stamp Act in 1766. Instead, Americans remembered the tyranny Britain had imposed on them and how Britain used taxes and regulation as a weapon against American businesses and consumers.[32] From this point forward, Americans viewed every new tax, rule, regulation, and policy as a means of oppression and an act of tyranny. As William Smith, Jr. of New York wrote of the Stamp Act: "This single stroke has lost Great Britain the affection of all her Colonies."[33]

While the Stamp Act inflamed the passions of the colonists, it also sparked a political debate regarding the nature of government. Colonists asked whether Britain had the right to raise taxes and impose laws upon the colonies. More so, they questioned whether Britain looked out for the colonists' interests or only acted for the benefit of the British government and those living in Britain. The colonists asked themselves whether Britain was their mother country or a despotic tyrant ruling over them.

Britain argued that, even though the colonists had no direct representation, they did have *virtual* representation and, therefore, Britain could tax them. Thomas Whately, the British Member of Parliament who drafted the Stamp Act, argued:

> The Colonies are in exactly the same Situation: All British Subjects are really in the same; none are actually, all are virtually represented in Parliament; for every Member of Parliament sits in the House, not as Representative of his own Constituents, but as one of that august Assembly by which the Commons of Great Britain are represented… The Colonies and all British Subjects whatever, have an equal Share in the general Representation of the Commons of Great Britain, and are bound by the Consent of the Majority of that House, whether their own particular Representatives consented to or opposed the Measures there taken, or whether they had or had not particular Representatives there.[34]

This argument was not good enough for the colonists. Even though five-sixths of British adult males also lacked the right to vote, Americans did not believe that they were *virtually* represented. They demanded actual representation in proportion to their population.[35]

After the repeal of the Stamp Act, Britain returned to indirect taxes on the colonies, such as import duties. However, these duties brought in just £45,000 per year in the late 1760s, only a tenth of the expense of defending the colonies.[36] If Britain desired to keep its American colonies, more taxes needed to be collected. Adam Smith argued in 1776, "The English colonists have never yet contributed any thing towards the defence of the mother country, or towards the support of its civil government. They themselves, on the contrary, have hitherto been defended almost entirely at the expence of the mother country."[37] Adam Smith even suggested to Britain that, if the colonies will not pay for their own defense and government, Britain should let them be free and independent.[38]

Britain tried again to raise the needed funds with the Townshend Acts of 1767. The Townshend Acts imposed new tariffs on a variety of goods that America did not produce and legally could only import from Britain. These tariffs were not much different from those that previously existed, but Americans saw them as replacements for the Stamp Act. Prior to the Stamp Act, the colonists largely ignored tariffs such as these and there were few protests against them. After the Stamp Act, every new tariff, no matter how insignificant, would be a reason to protest.

Responding to the new taxes, the Massachusetts House of Representatives formally petitioned the British government to have the Townshend Acts revoked. The Circular Letter written by Samuel Adams argued:

> The acts made there imposing Duties on the People of this province with the sole & express purpose of raising a Revenue, are Infringments of their natural & constitutional Rights because as they are not represented in the British Parliament His Majestys Commons in Britain by those Acts grant their Property without their consent. This House further are of Opinion, that their Constituents considering their local Circumstances cannot by any possibility be represented in the Parliament, & that it will forever be impracticable that they should be equally represented there & consequently not at all; being separated by an Ocean of a thousand leagues.[39]

Thus, Massachusetts rejected any taxation without representation and further argued that such representation was impossible. In other words, Britain had no right to impose taxes on the colonies for any reason without their approval. In response, Massachusetts Royal Governor Francis Bernard dissolved the Massachusetts House of Representatives. Deprived of their peaceful and lawful means of protest, the people took to the streets, attacked British officials, and boycotted British goods. Britain countered by cracking down on smuggling, including the capture of John Hancock's ship *Liberty*, and by sending thousands of troops to Boston. This only further inflamed the colonists, especially when British troops fired on a belligerent crowd on March 5, 1770, killing five people in the so-called Boston Massacre.

Britain repealed the Townshend Acts in 1770. The tariffs had brought in just £21,000 per year whereas the American boycott cost British businesses £700,000.[40] Britain let one tax remain "as a mark of the supremacy of Parliament, and an efficient declaration of their right to govern the colonies."[41] Although the tax on tea was low and only symbolic,[42] Americans saw this as another infringement on their rights and a violation of their "no taxation without representation" pledge. To avoid the tax, Americans smuggled in Dutch tea. The British fleet captured much of the smuggled tea coming into Boston, but the colonists successfully smuggled the tea into other ports, including New York City and Philadelphia, two of the colonies' largest cities.

The Tea Act's true purpose was not to raise revenue, but to stop the smuggling of Dutch tea and help save the financially troubled East India Company. The Tea Act refunded duties the East India Company paid to import and re-export tea into and out of Britain and gave the company permission to export tea directly from India to America without having to go through Britain. This gave the East India Company a virtual monopoly in America and even subsidized the company at the expense of American consumers.

Massachusetts merchants, shippers, and their employees led the fight against the Tea Act. A mob dressed as Indians boarded a British ship and threw the British tea into Boston Harbor. Britain was losing control of the colonies and was not quite sure what to do about it. Lord North,

Britain's Prime Minister, remarked, "Whatever may be the consequence, we must risk something; if we do not, all is over."[43]

MERCANTILISM

Even though taxes received the bulk of the attention, especially with the catchy slogan "no taxation without representation," mercantilism played an equally important role in Britain's American policy and the American Revolution. In fact, the Tea Act was primarily about protecting British economic interests and, likewise, the Boston Tea Party was an act of resistance against British mercantilist policies. The small tax on tea was a secondary consideration for both Britain and America.

For well over a century, Britain treated its colonies as a captive export market and a source of cheap natural resources. Focused on developing America's virtually unlimited land and abundant raw materials, the colonies had almost no industry. As a result, Americans spent nearly a third of their income on imported goods.[44] In effect, the colonists produced raw goods and shipped them to Britain to be converted into finished goods. Those finished products were then shipped back to America for the colonists to buy. At each step of the process, British manufacturers, shippers, and tax collectors made money at the expense of the colonists.

In the 1760s and 1770s, Britain strengthened its mercantilist policies to reduce America's competitiveness. Although most Americans made their living through farming, it was their maritime activities that most threatened British dominance. Massachusetts became a hub of fishing, whaling, and ship-building activities. Ninety percent of Massachusetts' exports to Europe and ten percent of America's were produced by the fishing industry.[45] These American fishermen competed with British fishing interests near Britain and Nova Scotia. Likewise, whaling became another profitable enterprise in Massachusetts, again competing with the British and Canadians.[46]

America needed many boats for its fishing and whaling industries and became quite adept at building them. By 1776, America had the third largest fleet in the world.[47] America had abundant lumber for ship building, which enabled New England to build ships at a cost 20 to 50 percent less than European builders.[48] America had become Britain's leading competitor in fishing, whaling, shipping, and ship building. As a result, New England and Britain often argued about trade, another reason the rebellion against British rule began in New England.

Furthermore, America started competing with Britain in manufactured goods, largely as a result of the trade dispute following the Stamp Act. Certainly, America could not yet compete for sales in Europe or Britain, but the colonists produced more of the metal, wood, and textile goods that they had been importing from Britain.

However, the British mercantilist policy began long before America competed with Britain. While Britain was fighting a civil war from 1642 to 1651, the Dutch took advantage of Britain's preoccupation with internal affairs and captured much of the trade with British America. To restore its trade advantage with its own colonies, the British Parliament passed the first Navigation Act in 1651, requiring all colonial trade be done by British or colonial ships, thereby excluding the Dutch and all other nations. This trade dispute led to a series of military conflicts: the Anglo-Dutch Wars of 1652 to 1654, 1665 to 1667, and 1672 to 1674.

The objective of mercantilism was not to generate tax revenue, though it did that as well. The primary purpose was to benefit British manufacturers by forcing the colonies to trade almost exclusively with Britain. Whether this was accomplished is questionable. The colonies circumvented the Navigation Acts as they smuggled goods and bribed officials to evade restrictions. This additional cost of doing business along with the risk of the British navy capturing smuggling ships made the Navigation Acts very unpopular in the colonies.

Britain designed its mercantilist policy to benefit British shipping interests by banning foreign ships from Britain and its colonies. While the Dutch built smaller, lighter, more efficient ships, the British built larger, heavier, more defensible ships that were slower, required a larger crew, and often had cannons on board for defense. Americans would have preferred using cheaper Dutch ships, but the British forced the colonies to use British ships. This also had the desired effect of strengthening the British navy because British merchant ships were well suited for war.

British consumers benefited as well. Britain required America to send all exports through British ports, making it easier and less costly for America to sell its goods to Britain than to the rest of Europe.

British mercantilism did help some colonists. American indigo producers benefited from market protection.[49] More significantly, New England's ship building and shipping industries profited by eliminating foreign competition.[50] Furthermore, by relying on the British navy for protection, Americans could build faster, less defensible ships that operated at half the expense of British ships. This helped produce a quadrupling of wage rates in the American shipping business.[51]

However, most American businesses and nearly all American consumers suffered because British mercantilism raised the price of imports.[52] In *A New Economic View of American History: From Colonial Times to 1940*, Jeremy Atack and Peter Passell summarize the costs of British mercantilism: "Americans paid higher prices and earned smaller incomes than would have been the case if they had been free to use the cheapest shipping service and ship by the most direct routing... In short, the Navigation Acts forced Americans to pay more and consume fewer imports and earn less and sell fewer exports."[53]

Nevertheless, the cost of British mercantilism was negligible. According to an analysis by Robert Thomas in *The Journal of Economic History*, the total burden of the Navigation Acts in 1770 was $2.66 million—about $1.24 per capita or 2 percent of income. However, Thomas estimates that British protection was worth $1.775 million. The net cost to America of British trade policy was just $885,000 or $0.41 per capita, less than one percent of income. Even then, Thomas admits "it is not at all improbable...that the estimated losses are too high." Robert Thomas concludes, "It is difficult to make a convincing case for exploitation out of these results."[54] Others estimate the burden could have been as high as three percent of income, but most likely somewhat lower.[55] A tax of just one to three percent of income to pay for defense, civil administration, and a ready market for American goods was not overly burdensome and in line with what Americans would pay in the first decades of the republic under the Constitution. Jeremy Attack and Peter Passell conclude "that the British presence was not a serious financial hardship to the colonists."[56]

Even though Americans despised the mercantilist system, it was the standard of the day rather than the exception. All nations with large overseas holdings, including Spain, Portugal, and France, enacted similar or even more burdensome mercantilist policies. Even the Dutch, who in theory supported free trade, established the Dutch East India Company to monopolize trade with its colonies. When the British took over New Amsterdam from the Dutch in 1664, renaming it New York in the process, the residents of that growing commercial center continued to trade as if nothing happened. President Theodore Roosevelt, in his book *New York*, argues that "the Dutch settlers…were gainers rather than losers by the change" and that "the colony…had simply exchanged the rule of a company for the rule of a duke."[57]

All major colonial powers practiced mercantilism during the eighteenth century. This concept was not challenged in earnest until 1776 when Adam Smith destroyed its ideological foundation in *The Wealth of Nations* and when the American colonies rebelled against Britain and its mercantilist policies. Nevertheless, British taxes and mercantilism were not particularly cruel or tyrannical. As Gordon Wood sums up in *The American Revolution: A History*, "A series of trade acts and tax levies do not seem to add up to a justification for independence. There was none of the legendary tyranny of history that had so often driven desperate peoples into rebellion."[58]

COLONIAL MONEY SHORTAGE

America suffered perpetual trade deficits because of Britain's mercantilist policies. Without any significant gold or silver mines to offset its trade imbalances, the colonies suffered from a constant shortage of gold and silver money. Furthermore, Britain banned the export of British coins to the colonies and prohibited the colonies from minting their own.

To conduct business, the American colonies used a variety of currencies. Colonists smuggled in Spanish, French, Dutch, and British coins. They also minted their own coins in violation of British law. Merchants often used bills of exchange with each other. In parts of the South, colonists used tobacco as money with warehouse receipts acting as banknotes. And nearly everywhere, colonial governments issued bills of credit.[59]

The jumble of unreliable and volatile money hurt the colonial economy. In *An Empire of Wealth: The Epic History of American Economic Power*, John Steele Gordon explains, "The costs of evaluating and converting as needed the various forms of money was a very considerable cost on the aborning American economy."[60]

The colonies printed too many bills of credit and their values declined. Paper money issued by Massachusetts lost about 88 percent of its value against wheat, 80 percent of its value against silver, and 77 percent against the Pound in London. Even worse, Rhode Island's money lost 93 percent of its value against the Pound. In contrast, Pennsylvania's money fell only 21 percent against the Pound, Virginia's just 12 percent, and New York's 11 percent.[61]

This was yet another reason New England led the way toward independence. New York, Pennsylvania, and Virginia had stable currencies, whereas New Englanders saw the value of their currency and paper wealth decline markedly. New Englanders blamed Britain and the lack of specie for this problem. While Britain shares in the blame for the harm caused by its mercantilist and monetary policies, the excessive printing of paper money by certain colonial governments was the primary cause of this devaluation.

To stop the monetary inflation in America, Britain passed the Currency Acts of 1751 and 1764, which revoked the legal tender status of colonial paper money. The colonists saw this as another attempt to infringe upon their rights, to deprive the colonies of all gold and silver specie, and to make America dependent on Britain for its money.

In 1766, Benjamin Franklin listed "the prohibition of making paper money among themselves" and the prohibition of "bringing of foreign gold and silver into the Colonies" as major reasons Americans had lost respect for the British Parliament.[62] However, not everybody thought this situation was bad for the American colonies. Adam Smith took the opposite position, arguing that the lack of gold and silver in America reflected the colonies' economic growth: "Their great demand for active and productive stock makes it convenient for them to have as little dead stock as possible; and disposes them upon that account to content themselves with a cheaper, though less commodious instrument of commerce than gold and silver... It is not because they are poor that their payments are irregular and uncertain; but because they are too eager to become excessively rich."[63]

Adam Smith added that this lack of gold and silver prevented the colonists from paying the taxes imposed by Britain: "The Americans, it has been said, indeed, have no gold or silver money; the interior commerce of the country being carried on by a paper currency, and the gold and silver which occasionally come among them being all sent to Great Britain in return for the commodities which they receive from us. But without gold and silver, it is added, there is no possibility of paying taxes. We already get all the gold and silver which they have. How is it possible to draw from them what they have not?"[64]

The colonists had lodged a similar complaint in the Declaration of Rights and Grievances back in 1765: "That the duties imposed by several late acts of Parliament...will be extremely burthensome and grievous, and, from the scarcity of specie, the payment of them absolutely impracticable."[65]

By depriving the American colonists of their ability to pay taxes, Britain helped foment opposition to taxation. When Britain sensed an unwillingness to pay taxes, rather than an inability, Britain imposed mercantilist policies, enacted new taxes, and sent officials to administer them. Thus, the shortage of money contributed to the chain of events that led to the American Revolution.

WESTWARD EXPANSION

Nearly all American colonists lived within a few miles of the Atlantic Ocean or along the rivers that flowed from the interior. As the population grew, new demand for land pushed the colonists farther up the rivers and deeper into the country. This expansion put Americans in conflict with the native Indians and often with the British government.

In 1676, a planter named Nathaniel Bacon, who arrived in Virginia just two years earlier, led a rebellion against the governor, who many saw as being too friendly toward the Indians. Bacon also argued for lower taxes and more voting rights for the colonists. This rebellion was both a military war against the Indians, in which dozens were killed, and a political war against the royal governor of the Virginia Colony.

Although Bacon claimed he was leading a rebellion to ensure the safety of the colonists, some claim he was seeking power for himself whereas others argue he was seeking independence from Britain a full century before the American Revolution.[66] Regardless of his motives, Bacon's angry mob of a few hundred men demonstrated the same revolutionary fervor that the colonists would use to win their independence a hundred years later. Bacon's Rebellion gave America its first glimpse into the power of the mob. Those in power, both the British rulers and the American upper class, realized the damage a small but energetic group of rebels could cause.

Upon regaining control, the large plantation owners consolidated their power. They moved away from using indentured servants brought over from Britain because these immigrants rebelled whenever they thought their rights were being violated. Instead, the plantations shifted to slave labor. These political leaders also opened the west to settlement to appease the protestors.[67]

In the very same year, the Indians and colonists of Massachusetts fought for control of Indian lands in King Philip's War. Hundreds of colonists and thousands of Indians were killed. Because Massachusetts was self-governing, the people and the colonial government worked together, while the British government objected. Afterward, Britain tried to rein in colonial power in Massachusetts, but the colonists opposed increased British control and the infringement of their sovereignty.

Nevertheless, these wars and rebellions were rare in the early colonial period. In fact, Britain encouraged westward expansion as it raced to settle the interior before the French move down from Canada or the Spanish come up from the Gulf of Mexico.

After its victory in the French and Indian War, Britain gained control over all of North America east of the Mississippi River. No longer in a race to settle the West and wanting to reduce its military expenditures, Britain issued the Proclamation of 1763, which banned the colonists from moving west. However, many colonists were already living on the other side of Britain's "line of demarcation." Americans simply ignored this ban and disregarded the treaties Britain made with the Indians.[68]

In 1767, George Washington, who owned land in the West, called the Proclamation of 1763 "a temporary expedient to quiet the minds of the Indians."[69] Washington knew it would be only be a matter of time before the colonists settled this land, putting them back in conflict with Britain over the line of demarcation and with the Indians on the other side. When this occurred just a few years later, Britain tried to establish a firmer line with the Quebec Act of 1774, but this further angered American settlers, land speculators, and traders.[70]

This restriction on westward expansion was another cause of the American Revolution and was listed among the grievances against King George III in the Declaration of Independence: "He has endeavored to prevent the population of these States... raising the conditions of new Appropriations of Lands." The Declaration of Independence also protests Britain's alleged incitement of Indians against the colonists: "He has...endeavoured to bring on the inhabitants of our frontiers, the merciless Indian Savages whose known rule of warfare, is an undistinguished destruction of all ages, sexes and conditions."

The western settlers were among the most vocal supporters of political reform and independence. Law and order was largely absent from the West. The British and colonial governments had virtually no presence in the newly inhabited areas. Throughout the 1760s, western settlers in various colonies rebelled against the ineffective and unresponsive eastern governments. The settlers petitioned for more representation, took up arms, killed Indians aligned with the government, and gained control over county courts. These people had no allegiance to the British or colonial governments. As a result, they took the law into their own hands and declared their independence from Britain because they were already independent in practice.[71]

SOVEREIGNTY

The issues of taxation, mercantilism, money, and westward expansion were all part of a larger issue: sovereignty. While Spain and France actively controlled their colonies, Britain administered its colonies with a more hands-off approach. Alexis de Tocqueville explains, "The English colonies, and this is one of the main causes of their prosperity, have always enjoyed greater personal freedom and political independence than the colonies of other nations; but nowhere was this principle of liberty more completely applied than in the states of New England."[72]

Over the years, disagreements arose between the colonists and the British government regarding sovereignty. For example, when the Virginia Assembly passed the Two Penny Act in 1758, the British Board of Trade revoked it the following year. This prompted Patrick Henry to pronounce that the King of England "had degenerated into a tyrant, and forfeited all right to his subjects' obedience."[73]

Despite a few such squabbles, for most of the colonial period, the issue of sovereignty was raised only in connection with the quarrels over taxation, mercantilism, money, and westward expansion. The Massachusetts Government Act of 1774 changed all that.

In response to the Boston Tea Party, Britain passed the Coercive Acts to compel America into paying for the destroyed tea and to force the colonists to submit to British rule. The colonists, however, dubbed them the Intolerable Acts and vigorously opposed them. George Washington called these acts "an Invasion of our Rights and Privileges."[74]

The Boston Port Act was the most direct response to the Boston Tea Party. This part of the Intolerable Acts shut down Boston harbor until the colonists paid for the destroyed tea. The colonists complained that Britain was penalizing them indiscriminately instead of punishing just those responsible. The Boston Port Act also had the ulterior motive of trying to divide the colonies. By attacking Boston alone, Britain hoped that other ports would benefit and thereby support the act.[75]

However, most Americans realized that if Britain could blockade Boston, it could blockade any American port. All of the colonies opposed the closing of the port of Boston out of fear, not solidarity. Tea coming into New York and Philadelphia was sent back to Britain. In Charleston, the tea was left to rot. Throughout the colonies, agents of the East India Company were threatened and forced to resign.[76]

The most politically damaging of the Intolerable Acts was the Massachusetts Government Act, which deprived the people of the self-government they had enjoyed for 150 years. Even though self-government in the colonies was limited and often neglected, it was held dear by the colonists.

In most of the colonies, the people elected very few government officials and Britain often had the power to reverse their decisions, as was the case with Virginia's Two Penny Act. Even in New England, where, according to Tocqueville, "this principle of liberty more completely applied,"[77] political leadership belonged to a small group of elites. In *A Defence of the Constitutions of Government of the United States of America*, John Adams explains, "Go into every village in New England, and you will find that the office of justice of the peace, and even the place of representative, which has ever depended only on the freest election of the people, have generally descended from generation to generation, in three or four families at most."[78]

Furthermore, the American colonists were not very enthusiastic about their right to vote. In New England, which was so upset when the British government took away their right to self-rule, just 25 percent of eligible men voted in the mid-1700s. Only 40 percent of eligible men voted in Virginia elections and between 20 and 40 percent voted in Pennsylvania and New York. Although turnout was higher in urban areas than in rural areas, it was low in both. Less than 10 percent of the people voted in rural South Carolina while 30 percent voted in Charleston.[79]

These voter turnouts may be low by modern standards, but they exceeded those in eighteenth-century Britain.[80] Furthermore, many people chose not to vote because elected officials had little power, especially in regions where the British government appointed the most powerful officials who then appointed the officials below them. Additionally, government in colonial America was tiny while taxes were negligible. To most people, it mattered little who ran for office and who won.

Nevertheless, the denial of local sovereignty through the Massachusetts Government Act angered the people as no other act had done before. The angry mobs stepped up their protests and called for rebellion, but only to restore their rights as British citizens. The Declaration of Independence lists British interference in colonial self-government as a major cause of the revolution:

> He has dissolved Representative Houses repeatedly, for opposing with manly firmness his invasions on the rights of the people.

> He has obstructed the Administration of Justice by refusing his Assent to Laws for establishing Judiciary Powers.

> For taking away our Charters, abolishing our most valuable Laws and altering fundamentally the Forms of our Governments.

> For suspending our own Legislatures, and declaring themselves invested with power to legislate for us in all cases whatsoever.

Nevertheless, few people called for independence in 1774. Most Americans, including many in Massachusetts and certainly most in the other colonies, still would have liked to reconcile their differences with Britain.

Britain saw the colonial rebellion differently. In November 1774, King George III wrote to British Prime Minister Lord North: "The New England Governments are in a state of rebellion, blows must decide whether they are to be subject to this country or independent."[81] Britain's response to American protests would push even more Americans toward rebellion, revolution, and independence.

BRITISH TYRANNY

The disputes over taxes, mercantilism, money, westward expansion, and sovereignty were reasons for petitions, boycotts, riots, and small-scale rebellions. However, none of them produced revolution, except possibly the issue of sovereignty in Massachusetts. What really incited the masses and pushed the Founding Fathers toward independence was the encouragement of slave rebellions in the South and the destruction of American cities in late 1775 and early 1776.

In June 1775, the British set fire to Charlestown, Massachusetts, during the Battle of Bunker Hill. In October 1775, the British set ablaze the town of Falmouth, Maine. In January 1776, the British burned down most of Norfolk, Virginia. In all cases, the British were trying to quell rebellions, but their actions were disproportionate to the colonists' opposition, which primarily involved capturing ships and weapons. Furthermore, by destroying entire towns, the British were punishing the innocent along with the guilty.

To counter the growing rebellion in the South, Britain incited slaves against their owners. In November 1775, the Royal Governor of Virginia, Lord Dunmore, offered freedom to all slaves willing to fight for the British. As Thomas Jefferson wrote in the Declaration of Independence, "He has excited domestic insurrections amongst us."

In fact, slaves started fleeing their owners and fighting for the British even before Lord Dunmore's offer.[82] The South feared half a million slaves fighting against them. James Madison later wrote, "I take no notice of an unhappy species of population abounding in some of the States, who, during the calm of regular government, are sunk below the level of men; but who, in the tempestuous scenes of civil violence, may emerge into the human character, and give a superiority of strength to any party with which they may associate themselves."[83]

Prior to Lord Dunmore's offer to free the slaves, Virginia did not actively support Massachusetts in its fight against the British. When the British threatened to upset the peace and Southern way of life, many in the South started supporting the war against British tyranny.

Inciting slave rebellions against the South and destroying the colonists' homes and businesses were direct attacks on the people's lives and livelihoods. No longer would the rebels throw tea overboard, chase government officials away, or simply seize enemy ships and weapons. The colonists started the War for Independence because Britain was already waging war against them.

AMERICAN SUPERIORITY

By destroying American towns and revoking colonial sovereignty, Britain sought to demonstrate its superiority. However, Americans increasingly saw themselves as superior to the British. In many respects, the colonists were correct.

In the middle and late 1700s, new jobs and opportunities developed in the colonies. Fishing and whaling were big businesses. Manufacturing was increasing rapidly. Merchants were getting rich in the lucrative shipping business. However, most colonists worked in agriculture. With a virtually unlimited amount of land, plentiful lumber, navigable rivers, and diverse climates, American farmers could provide for themselves and produce surpluses to trade for other goods.

Even in the colonial period, the American people earned more on average, had better diets, and were more literate than those in Britain and the rest of Europe. Even though American men earned more money than those doing similar work in England, America was still able to produce more cheaply because of the abundance of land and material. As a result, Americans likely had a standard of living twenty percent higher than the British[84] and America had a proportionately larger middle class than any other Western country.[85] With higher incomes and plenty of fertile farmland, Americans had better diets than their British cousins and, as a result, were a few inches taller, on average, than their British counter-parts.[86] Furthermore, the mortality rate in America was twenty to thirty percent lower than in Britain.[87]

By the time of the American Revolution, Americans had settled a land area 50 percent larger than Britain.[88] Britain had about 11 million people, compared with America's 2.5 million, of which 500,000 were slaves. This made each American extremely land rich in comparison to the British people. Even though the colonial economy was still 60 percent smaller than Britain's in 1775, it had grown 500 percent in the previous fifty years, compared with a 25 percent increase in Britain.[89]

Whites in America were more literate than those in Britain.[90] Seventy percent of men and 45 percent of women in New England were literate in 1750. In the South, 50 to 60 percent of men and 40 percent of women were literate.[91] This relatively high rate of literacy enabled Americans to read newspapers that reported and analyzed the events of the day. Consequently, pamphlets such as Thomas Paine's *Common Sense* had a great impact on American thinking.

On average, white Southerners were more than twice as wealthy as Northern whites. Even excluding slaves, the average white Southerner still had 60 percent more wealth than the average white person in the North.[92] Additionally, wealth inequality among free people in New England was greater than that in the South or Middle Colonies. In fact, the poorest people in New England were heavily indebted while those in the rest of the colonies were nearly debt free.[93] Farming was difficult in New England because the land was often rocky, the soil thin, and the growing season short. Many New England farmers struggled and debt overwhelmed quite a few. The resulting inequality within New England and between the North and the South was another key reason the revolution began in New England.

Nevertheless, the opportunities America provided and the success many achieved fueled massive influxes of immigrants and promoted natural population growth. Between 1750 and 1770, the American population nearly doubled.[94] British and non-British immigrants escaped from poor economic conditions in Europe and sought better lives in America. To those who succeeded, America was better than their places of origin. These immigrants could not understand why America had to be subservient to Britain.

One recent arrival from Britain also believed in American superiority. Thomas Paine argued throughout *Common Sense* that America was superior to Britain, that Americans were superior to the British, and that the colonies would be more prosperous independent of British rule.[95] Furthermore, Paine persuaded many Americans that their superiority would enable them to beat the British army in a war for independence.[96] Thus, the publication of *Common Sense* in January 1776 launched the American Revolution, despite its naïve proposal for the creation of a new government. As John Adams complained to Thomas Jefferson more than 40 years later: "What a poor, ignorant, malicious, short-sighted, crapulous mass is Tom Paine's "Common

Sense"... And yet history is to ascribe the American Revolution to Thomas Paine!"[97]

REBELLION

The rebellion against Britain was not instigated by a single issue like taxes, mercantilism, monetary policy, westward expansion, or sovereignty. John Adams argues that the "real American Revolution" was a "change in the principles, opinions, sentiments, and affections of the people."[98] He adds that "the Revolution was in the minds and hearts of the people."[99] Thus, the "real American Revolution" was about ideology *and* passion.

Along with his logical arguments against monarchy and the divine right of kings, Thomas Paine litters *Common Sense* with appeals to "affections," "feelings," and "passions."[100] In *American Insurgents, American Patriots*, T.H. Breen explains how these "passions" affected the colonists' thinking: "The argument is not that the insurgents did not have ideas about politics. They did. But these were ideas driven by immediate passions; they were amplified through fear, fury, and resentment."[101] As a result, Edmund Burke observed, "This fierce spirit of liberty is stronger in the English colonies probably than in any other people of the earth."[102]

This union of ideology and passion pushed the colonists to extremism. Anti-British sentiment was turned into opposition against all forms of government. When attacking the British government in *Common Sense*, Thomas Paine also rebuked government more generally as "a punisher" and "a necessary evil."[103]

When Britain lost control over the colonies, anarchy and chaos took over. The colonists formed new governments, but these were often too democratic and suffered from the shortcomings one would expect from hastily planned and ill-conceived political systems. The angry mobs overthrew governments, but lacked the knowledge, experience, and forethought to establish proper replacements.

Caught up in the emotion of revolution, the Patriots did not have the time nor the patience for details. They were too busy changing the world. As Thomas Paine wrote in *Common Sense*, "We have it in our power to begin the world over again. A situation similar to the present, hath not happened since the days of Noah."[104] In such an instance, the American people rushed to accomplish their goals without preparing for what lay ahead. The angry mobs rushed to overthrow British rule, but had no plan to replace it.

The American Revolution against British domination, injustice, oppression, and tyranny had begun; but peace, law, and order had been sacrificed at the altar of the angry mobs. The angry mobs started the revolution, but to win the war and the peace would require the help and leadership of a different set of men. These men were also Patriots with the same goals of liberty and limited government, but they had very different ideas of how to achieve their objectives.

CHAPTER TWO

FOUNDING FATHERS
IN COLONIAL AMERICA

While the angry mobs protested, boycotted, demanded
independence, and finally waged battle against British
tyranny, the men who would later be known as the Founding Fathers took a more cautious approach. These men, especially those
from the South, were very different from the rebels protesting against
British rule up in New England. Whereas the angry mobs could easily
disband and hide, these Founding Fathers publicly announced their
treason against Britain—a country and government they had previously
loved—when they pledged their lives, fortunes, and sacred honor to the
cause of independence.[1]

CONSERVATIVE LIBERALS

The signers of the Declaration of Independence, as a group, were
wealthier and better educated than the rest of America. Some inherited
their wealth whereas others earned it. Those not particularly wealthy
were still at the top of their fields, usually in law or politics. All these men
were hardworking and intelligent, regardless of their backgrounds. Alexis
de Tocqueville describes one group of Founding Fathers in *Democracy in
America*: "The greater landowners to the south of the Hudson consti-
tuted a superior class, having ideas and tastes of its own and, in general,
encompassing all political action in the center. It was a sort of aristocracy
hardly distinguishable from the mass of the people whose enthusiasms
and interests it readily embraced... This was the class which headed the
revolt in the South and which gave to the American revolution its
greatest men."[2]

Eighteenth-century Britain was both conservative and liberal. Britain was conservative with its constitutional monarchy and traditional system of peerage and honours. Britain was also the most liberal nation in the world, with the people's rights guaranteed by the Magna Carta. This conservative-liberal synthesis was brought over to the colonies, where it flourished for more than a century. Edmund Burke explains that the American colonists were "not only devoted to liberty, but to liberty according to English ideas, and on English principles."[3]

Unlike most revolutions, the goal of the American Revolution was not to change society. In fact, the Founders and most Americans fought to maintain society as it was. The Declaration of Independence opens with:

> When, in the course of human events, it becomes necessary for one people to dissolve the political bands which have connected them with another...

With the Declaration of Independence, America was dissolving the political bands connecting it to Britain. America was not dissolving the bands that held its society together. Not once does the Declaration of Independence mention society or changing the social system. One Founding Father even lamented that, amid the chaos of the revolution, "For the want of civil government the bands of society are totally dis-united, and the people...have become perfectly savage."[4] This destruction of the bands of society is not what the Founding Fathers wanted and they worked hard to prevent it.

If Britain were to overthrow its monarchical government, that would be a radical change in its society. However, for Americans, who had no inherited classes or titles, dissolving the political bands between Britain and America would leave society virtually untouched. Although the signers of the Declaration of Independence could not be considered conservative from a British viewpoint, they certainly were from an American perspective.

These leading men were also liberal in the classical sense of "a commitment to the liberty of individual citizens," "the proper role of just government as the protection of the liberties of individual citizens," and "a commitment to a system of free markets."[5] As Frederick Douglass said about the signers of the Declaration of Independence: "They loved their country better than their own private interests… In their admiration of liberty, they lost sight of all other interests… They believed in order; but not in the order of tyranny."[6]

Therein lay the delicate balance. The Founding Fathers wished to protect the liberties of the American colonists and stop British tyranny while still maintaining law and order.

BENEFITS OF BRITISH COLONIALISM

While Thomas Paine argued that American superiority was a reason to declare independence, there were many who argued that America became great under Britain and would become even greater under continued British supervision. In the end, the debate was not about whether America was doing well under British rule, but whether it would do better or worse on its own.

The Founding Fathers recognized that America received many benefits from its connection with Britain, most notably a ready export market for American goods. Adam Smith points out that "the English colonies have been more favoured, and have been allowed a more extensive market, than those of any other European nation"[7] and "with regard to the importation of goods from Europe, England has likewise dealt more liberally with her colonies than any other nation."[8]

Because of this favored status, along with Britain's mercantilist policies, approximately half of American exports went to Britain and Ireland with other British colonies adding to that total.[9] Exports to Britain doubled between 1762 and 1775.[10] America also received 75 percent of its imports from Britain.[11]

This trade enabled America to become an international shipping power. In fact, shipping likely produced a greater profit for America than any commodity, even tobacco.[12] The British navy protected American shipping while Britain's mercantilist policies, which prohibited non-British ships from trading with the colonies, subsidized both British and

American shipping interests. Revolution and independence risked this profitable endeavor.

Although Adam Smith shattered the intellectual basis for mercantilism in *The Wealth of Nations*, the British system was not all bad. First, Adam Smith explained the problem with mercantilism: "To prohibit a great people, however, from making all that they can of every part of their own produce, or from employing their stock and industry in the way that they judge most advantageous to themselves, is a manifest violation of the most sacred rights of mankind."[13] Despite the problems caused by mercantilism, Adam Smith added, "Unjust, however, as such prohibitions may be, they have not hitherto been very hurtful to the colonies."[14] In the end, Adam Smith determined, "In every thing, except their foreign trade, the liberty of the English colonists to manage their own affairs their own way is complete."[15]

In fact, the British Empire succeeded not just because of its powerful navy and its mercantilist policies, but also because of its division of labor, an idea that was gaining prominence in the late eighteenth century as an essential economic concept. Within the British Empire, Britain specialized in textiles and manufacturing, Quebec in furs, New England in fishing, shipping, and ship building, the Mid-Atlantic in farming, the South in tobacco, the Deep South in rice and indigo, the West Indies in sugar, and India in cotton. This system made America reliant on British manufactured goods, but also made Britain reliant on American commodities.

The result was that, on average, colonial Americans were among the wealthiest people of their day. They were also the freest people in the world. For these reasons, many Americans wished to keep their political connection with Britain, though they recognized certain aspects needed repair. In *A New Economic View of American History: From Colonial Times to 1940*, Jeremy Atack and Peter Passell explain, "On the eve of the Revolution America was experiencing rapid extensive growth... The Revolution, however, plunged the country into a new and uncertain political and economic environment."[16] In the face of this uncertainty, the Founding Fathers were understandably and wisely cautious.

A CAUTIOUS APPROACH

Besides the economic risk entailed in revolution and independence, the Founding Fathers worried about exposure to other dangers. The most obvious and pressing concern was the war. Britain had the most powerful army and navy in the world. Britain had already demonstrated the kind of destruction it could inflict on America at Charlestown, Falmouth, and Norfolk. While the angry mobs were quick to attack Britain, the Founding Fathers feared Britain's response.

Furthermore, the Founding Fathers were afraid that if the colonies declared independence, Britain might return Florida to Spain and Canada to France if those nations agreed not to ally with America. Then, France or Spain could have attacked America seeking territorial gains during or after the War for Independence.[17] Indian tribes could have also used this opportunity to attack the embattled American states.

Most of all, the Founding Fathers feared anarchy. As the angry mobs rebelled against Britain, British colonial governments lost control and anarchy became commonplace. One mob in May 1775 attacked Myles Cooper, president of King's College, today's Columbia University, for his loyalty to Britain. Alexander Hamilton, a twenty-year old college student who was already an outspoken supporter of the revolution, saved Cooper's life and denounced the "passions" of "the unthinking populace" and their "disregard of all authority."[18] Hamilton was one of the most ambitious and vocal supporters of the revolution, yet even he realized the importance of law and order during this chaotic time.

John Adams was another early supporter of the revolution, yet he too worried about its effects. John Adams was a prominent opponent of the Stamp Act, arguing that Englishmen could be taxed only if they were represented in government. After a dispute in 1772 over who would pay and thereby control the judges of Massachusetts, John Adams argued that if "no Line that can be drawn between the Supreme Authority of Parliament and the total Independence of the Colonies" then "the Consequence is, either that the Colonies are the Vassals of the Parliament, or, that they are totally independent. As it cannot be supposed to have been the Intention of the Parties in the Compact, that we should be reduced to a State of Vassallage, the Conclusion is, that it was their Sense, that we were thus Independent."[19]

Even though Adams was an early advocate of revolution and independence, he realized America must progress slowly to give the laggards a chance to catch up to forward thinkers like himself. He wrote to his wife in June 1775, "America is a great, unwieldy body. Its progress must be slow. It is like a large fleet sailing under convoy. The fleetest sailors must wait for the dullest and slowest. Like a coach and six, the swiftest horses must be slackened, and the slowest quickened, that all may keep an even pace."[20] Adams recognized that without unity, the revolution would fail. Though Massachusetts was ready for revolution, in fact it was already occurring, the rest of the country still had to catch up.

Like Hamilton, John Adams supported the revolution but worried about the loss of law and order. While Adams advocated "that the exercise of every kind of authority under the said crown should be totally suppressed" and that the people should defend "their lives, liberties, and properties, against the hostile invasions and cruel depredations of their enemies," he also hoped "for the preservation of internal peace, virtue, and good order."[21] As he was helping draft the Declaration of Independence on July 3, 1776, Adams wrote to his wife that he was "well aware of the toil, and blood, and treasure, that it will cost us to maintain this declaration, and support and defend these States."[22] Although John Adams was an early advocate of independence and a leading proponent of revolution, as a member of Congress, he worked hard to maintain peace, law, and order during this chaotic time.

Samuel Adams, second cousin to John Adams, was another well-known and early opponent of British oppression. Back in 1764, Samuel Adams opposed the Sugar Act, arguing, "For if our Trade may be taxed why not our Lands? Why not the Produce of our Lands & every thing we possess or make use of? This we apprehend annihilates our Charter Right to govern & tax ourselves—It strikes at our Brittish Privileges, which as we have never forfeited them, we hold in common with our Fellow Subjects who are Natives of Brittain: If Taxes are laid upon us in any shape without our having a legal Representation where they are laid, are we not reduced from the Character of free Subjects to the miserable State of Tributary Slaves?"[23] In 1771, Samuel Adams explained, "We have all the liberties and immunities of Englishmen… It is our duty therefore to contend for them whenever attempts are made to violate them."[24] Sam Adams then served in the Continental Congress, advocated independence, and signed the Declaration of Independence. For more than a decade leading up to the American Revolution, Samuel Adams was a constant opponent of British oppression and a stalwart defender of the colonists' "Brittish Privileges."

Nevertheless, even Samuel Adams was cautious when it came to rebelling against Britain. Samuel Adams pointed out in 1768 that "the peace and good order of the province has been greatly interrupted by Riots and Tumults, when in all probability ninety-nine in a hundred never heard of it, and of those who had ninety-nine in a hundred detested it… I am no friend to "Riots, Tumults and unlawful Assemblies"… But they are in the right of it to complain, and complain ALOUD. And they will complain, till they are either redress'd, or become poor deluded miserable ductile Dupes, fitted to be made the slaves of dirty tools of arbitrary power."[25]

In a very prescient letter written in January 1773, eleven months before the Boston Tea Party, Samuel Adams explained his fear of what might occur and his hope to prevent it: "I have long feard that this unhappy Contest between Britain & America will end in Rivers of Blood; Should that be the Case, America I think may wash her hands in Innocence; yet it is the highest prudence to prevent if possible so dreadful a Calamity."[26] This so-called rabble rouser, who supposedly gave the signal that started the Boston Tea Party, was actually a man who desired peace, feared the angry mobs of his home state, and dreaded British retaliation.

Benjamin Franklin also feared revolution. As early as 1754, Benjamin Franklin sought to avoid conflict with Britain through his Albany Plan, which was "a plan for the union of all the colonies under one government, so far as might be necessary for defence, and other important general purposes." After the American Revolution ended, Franklin wrote about this plan: "I am still of opinion it would have been happy for both sides, if it had been adopted. The colonies so united would have been sufficiently strong to have defended themselves: there would then have been no need of troops from England, of course the subsequent pretext for taxing America; and the bloody contest it occasioned, would have been avoided: but such mistakes are not new: history is full of errors of states and princes."[27]

In 1766, ten years before the Declaration of Independence, Benjamin Franklin warned Britain that America was slowly moving toward independence and that Britain should appease the colonists or risk losing them. Franklin wrote, "The time has been, when the colonies would have esteemed it a great advantage, as well as honor to be permitted to send members to Parliament; and would have asked for that privilege, if they could have had the least hopes of obtaining it. The time is now come, when they are indifferent about it, and will probably not ask it, though they might accept it if offered them; and the time will come, when they will certainly refuse it. But if such a union were now established (which methinks it highly imports this country to establish) it would probably subsist as long as Britain shall continue as a nation."[28]

Franklin laid much of the blame for the increased tensions between America and Britain on the angry mobs. In March 1773, Benjamin Franklin argued that it would be best "to keep our people quiet" because Britain used the "insurrections" as "a good pretence for increasing the military among us, and putting us under more severe restraints."[29] That same month, Franklin pointed out that America should wait patiently and peacefully because "by our rapidly increasing strength we shall soon become of so much importance, that none of our just claims or privileges will be, as heretofore, unattended to, nor any security we can wish for our rights be denied us."[30]

Less than a year later, Franklin condemned the actions of the angry mob at the Boston Tea Party. He called it an "act of violent injustice on our part" and admitted that he was "truly concern'd, as I believe all considerate Men are with you, that there should seem to any a Necessity for carrying Matters to such Extremity, as, in a Dispute about Publick Rights, to destroy private Property."[31]

While representing Pennsylvania in London, Franklin became disillusioned by the corruption in the British government when officials offered him bribes in exchange for supporting taxes on the colonies. Recognizing that there was nothing he could do in Britain to maintain the peace, he returned home to Philadelphia to help shape events in the colonies. Franklin returned to America in May 1775, just sixteen days after the Battles of Lexington and Concord. Franklin announced that reconciliation with Britain was impossible,[32] a conclusion he probably reached even before the recent conflicts.

In July 1775, Franklin presented his Articles of Confederation and Perpetual Union to the Second Continental Congress, which, in effect, would have been a declaration of independence. Franklin knew that there was not yet enough support for independence, so he read it to the Congress but did not even request a vote. Franklin knew the country still needed more unity if it were to fulfill its destiny. So he waited for the rest of the country to catch up to him.

While Franklin favored independence in July 1775, Thomas Jefferson still did not. In the first draft of the Declaration on Taking Up Arms of July 1775, Jefferson wrote, "We mean not in any wise to affect that union with them in which we have so long & so happily lived & which we wish so much to see again restored."[33] Jefferson even argued in August 1775 that America "would rather be in dependence on Great Britain, properly limited, than on any nation upon earth, or than on no nation."[34] He was one of many who supported reconciliation with Britain but, at the same time, he recognized certain changes to the current systems of government and trade needed fixing.

George Washington was also adamant about defending the rights of the colonists. In 1769, he noted how America's protests fell on deaf ears in London, but "that something should be done to avert the stroke, and maintain the liberty, which we have derived from our ancestors. But the manner of doing it, to answer the purpose effectually, is the point in question… Yet arms, I would beg leave to add, should be the last resource, the dernier resort." Washington proposed "starving their trade and manufactures" as a means of protesting and attacking Britain peacefully.[35] After the Boston Tea Party, Washington expressed approval of their cause but not their methods: "The cause of Boston…ever will be considered as the cause of America (not that we approve their conduct in destroying the Tea)."[36]

Washington only embraced military tactics after the Battles of Lexington and Concord, though he was saddened by this necessity: "Unhappy it is, though, to reflect, that a brother's sword has been sheathed in a brother's breast, and that the once happy and peaceful plains of America are either to be drenched in blood, or inhabited by slaves. Sad alternative! But can a virtuous man hesitate in his choice?"[37]

Even Thomas Paine admitted that he was a strong supporter of reconciliation prior to the Battles of Lexington and Concord: "No man was a warmer wisher for reconciliation than myself, before the fatal nineteenth of April 1775, but the moment the event of that day was made known, I rejected the hardened, sullen tempered Pharaoh of England for ever; and disdain the wretch, that with the pretended title of father of his people, can unfeelingly hear of their slaughter, and composedly sleep with their blood upon his soul."[38] Though Americans had been protesting against British taxes and mercantilism for a decade and angry mobs had been causing chaos for years, prior to the Battles of Lexington and Concord, Paine still thought that Britain and America could settle their differences. Only when the war had already begun, did Paine take up the cause of independence.

The Founding Fathers recognized that Britain was depriving Americans of their British rights. However, most of the Founders, even many of those considered instigators of the revolution, urged caution because they feared anarchy and British reprisals. The Founding Fathers took up arms only after they exhausted all other options and it became obvious that Britain would not grant America representation in Parliament or repeal its intolerable acts. After years of mob violence, George Washington and the Continental Congress finally went to war against Britain, but at the same time they worked to maintain law and order in a largely chaotic and anarchic country.

THE CONTINENTAL CONGRESS

In September and October 1774, delegates from all the colonies except Georgia met in Philadelphia for the First Continental Congress to discuss and decide how to respond to the Intolerable Acts, which shut down the port of Boston and revoked the sovereignty of Massachusetts. While certain delegates, including Patrick Henry, wished to declare independence and establish a new government, most supported reconciliation with Britain.

Congress decided to support opposition to the Intolerable Acts while recommending the colonists "conduct themselves peaceably…as far as can possibly be consistent with their immediate safety, and the security of the town; avoiding & discountenancing every violation of his Majesty's property, or any insult to his troops, and that they peaceably and firmly persevere in the line they are now conducting themselves, on the defensive."[39]

The First Continental Congress recommended a boycott of British goods starting in December 1774 as the best means of protest. The Continental Congress also planned to block all exports to Britain starting in September 1775, if Britain had not yet repealed the Intolerable Acts. However, these trade restrictions did not have time to work prior to the Battles of Lexington and Concord in April 1775, after which trade between Britain and America disappeared completely.

At the same time, the Continental Congress sent word "to the people of Great-Britain" that they should "place us in the same situation that we were at the close of the last war, and our harmony will be restored."[40] Furthermore, the Continental Congress protested against the "parliamentary taxes" imposed on the colonies with the "pretence of defraying the expense of government, and supporting the administration of justice, and defending, protecting, and securing the Colonies." Instead, the Continental Congress informed the British government that America could tax, administer, and defend itself.[41]

At the conclusion of the First Continental Congress, the delegates agreed to meet for a second congress in May 1775, but only if it were needed. Most delegates believed Britain and the colonies would reconcile their differences by then and a Second Continental Congress would be unnecessary.[42]

In November 1774, King George III wrote to British Prime Minister Lord North that "the New England Governments are in a state of rebellion, blows must decide whether they are to be subject to this country or independent."[43] However, there was still an influential element within Britain that supported America in its cause and argued for reconciliation. Among this group were Edmund Burke, a leading Whig and member of the British House of Commons, and Sir William Blackstone, a leading Tory and the judge who wrote the influential *Commentaries on the Laws of England*.[44] The Continental Congress hoped these men and the economic impact of their boycott would convince Britain to reconcile with the colonies.

On April 19, 1775, the first significant armed battles of the War for Independence took place at Lexington and Concord. Even after these battles, most American political leaders continued to push for reconciliation. Joseph Warren, a Boston doctor who served as president of the Massachusetts Provincial Congress and later died fighting the British in the Battle of Bunker Hill, was one of many who still believed in reconciliation. On April 26, 1775, on the heels of the Battles of Lexington and Concord, this Patriot wrote "to the Inhabitants of Great Britain" that "we profess to be his loyal and dutiful subjects," though "to the persecution and tyranny of his cruel ministry, we will not tamely submit... we determine to die or be free." Warren concludes, "We sincerely hope…we shall soon be altogether a free and happy people."[45]

In contrast to America's continued requests for reconciliation, the British government wanted to punish the rebels. Britain tried to arrest the rebel leaders, but the angry mobs were simply too large, well armed, and adept at guerilla-style combat for the British army.[46] As a result, the British suffered greater losses in these conflicts than did the colonial forces, further encouraging the rebels.

Delegates from all thirteen colonies gathered in Philadelphia on May 10, 1775 for the Second Continental Congress. While the Battles of Lexington and Concord convinced many rebels, such as Thomas Paine, that reconciliation was no longer possible, the Second Continental Congress raised the question of independence on May 16, but none argued for it. Instead, all the delegates favored reconciliation, though they disagreed on how best to approach it, what they would demand from Britain, and how likely they were to succeed.[47]

However, the main decision in front of the Second Continental Congress was not independence, but the war with Britain that had already begun. The Battles of Lexington and Concord occurred a month earlier. On the day that the Second Continental Congress first met, Benedict Arnold and Ethan Allen captured Fort Ticonderoga. Arnold acted under the auspices of the Massachusetts Committee of Safety while Allen and his Green Mountain Boys acted of their own volition. The British saw the attack on their fort as an offensive move by the colonies, but the Continental Congress tried to spin the news by arguing that it was an act of defense against invasion from Canada.[48]

On June 15, 1775, the Second Continental Congress chose George Washington to be commander-in-chief of the Continental Army, which had been established only the previous day. Until this point, all fighting was done by state militias or by volunteer groups, such as Ethan Allen's Green Mountain Boys. The Continental Congress decided it was time for an organized and disciplined army. As George Washington argued, "To place any dependence upon militia is assuredly resting upon a broken staff. Men just dragged from the tender scenes of domestic life, unaccustomed to the din of arms, totally unacquainted with every kind of military skill…are timid and ready to fly from their own shadows… The jealousy of a standing army, and the evils to be apprehended from one, are remote, and, in my judgment, situated and circumstanced as we are, not at all to be dreaded; but the consequence of wanting one, according to my ideas formed from the present view of things, is certain and inevitable ruin."[49]

Congress chose George Washington to lead the war effort not just for his military experience. John Adams nominated Washington to cement a bond between Massachusetts, the colony leading America into war, and Virginia, the most populous colony in America. This act showed both Massachusetts and Britain that all the colonies stood together. Furthermore, by choosing a Virginian to lead the war, the Second Continental Congress hoped to temper the fanaticism of Massachusetts while, at the same time, engender more American patriotism among Virginians and other Southerners. Whether America was to reconcile or declare independence, the Founding Fathers recognized they would be in a stronger position if the colonies were united.

On June 17, 1775, while Washington traveled to Massachusetts to take control of the army, British troops attacked fortifications on Bunker

Hill and Breed's Hill just outside Boston. Though the British technically won this battle by taking the heights and forcing the Americans to retreat to Cambridge, British casualties outnumbered American losses by more than two to one.[50] This gave the colonists hope that they could defeat the British in battle and win their independence. It also scared the British into thinking they could lose the war or that victory might come at great cost.

Following the victorious Battle of Ticonderoga, Ethan Allen and Benedict Arnold proposed invading Canada. Congress had no desire to do so and even ordered Allen and Arnold to abandon the forts they captured in upstate New York. After Allen and Arnold protested the orders, the Continental Congress relented on both issues. However, Congress chose General Philip Schuyler to lead the invasion of Canada "to promote the peace and security of these Colonies," but only "if General Schuyler finds it practicable, and that it will not be disagreeable to the Canadians."[51]

The Continental Congress knew that an invasion of Canada could not possibly promote peace and be agreeable to Canada, but it also realized that Ethan Allen and his Green Mountain Boys along with the Massachusetts militia under Benedict Arnold could invade Canada without Congress's consent. By agreeing to the invasion and by putting Schuyler in command instead of Arnold or Allen, Congress hoped that Schuyler would conduct the invasion in a more sensible manner. Just like choosing George Washington to lead the war, the Second Continental Congress chose Schuyler to moderate the fanaticism of Allen, Arnold, and their troops. The creation of the Continental Army was not just to defeat the British, but also to prevent undisciplined militias from starting foolish battles or turning into angry mobs.

Even though the Continental Congress and George Washington were now officially directing the war effort, they continued to seek reconciliation with Britain. In July 1775, the Second Continental Congress approved the Olive Branch Petition, in which Congress argued that the colonies were still loyal to the king but asked him to stop the cruel actions by his ministers. Despite America's entreaty, Britain moved in the opposite direction. In August 1775, King George

III issued his Proclamation of Rebellion, declaring that the colonies were in "open and avowed rebellion, by arraying themselves in a hostile manner, to withstand the execution of the law, and traitorously preparing, ordering and levying war against us." He vowed "to bring the traitors to justice."[52] King George III reiterated this in October when he said the colonies "manifestly carried on for the purpose of establishing an independent Empire."[53] Both houses of Parliament voted in agreement and Britain prohibited all trade with the American colonies until the rebellion ended.[54]

Even after this, America was still not ready to declare independence. New York, New Jersey, Pennsylvania, Maryland, and North Carolina still opposed breaking away from Britain. Many colonists, if not most, who supported the war in 1775 did so not to achieve total independence but to pressure Britain into granting them more autonomy within the British Empire.[55] Most of the delegates in the Second Continental Congress still favored reconciliation and the few who favored independence were not yet willing to use that word in public.[56] John Adams recalled other delegates to the Second Continental Congress telling him, "You must not utter the word independence, nor give the least hint or insinuation of the idea, either in Congress or any private conversation; if you do, you are undone; for the idea of independence is as unpopular in Pennsylvania, and in all the Middle and Southern States, as the Stamp Act itself. No man dares to speak of it."[57] Though they were not yet ready to declare independence, the Continental Congress defended the rebellion, issued formal protests against British oppression, and directed the war against Britain.[58]

On January 9, 1776, the very same day that Thomas Paine published *Common Sense*, James Wilson proposed rebutting King George III's charge that the colonists aimed for independence. Samuel Adams and the New England delegates blocked this attempt to reconcile with Britain. A second attempt a few weeks later received more support, but it too failed.[59] Nevertheless, the numbers were shifting. In 1775, nobody would even mention the word *independence*.[60] By early 1776, many delegates spoke of independence and a number of states and towns issued their own declarations of independence.[61]

By May 1776, the Continental Congress had moved very much toward independence. The publication of *Common Sense* in January certainly swayed many to the cause. The British evacuation from Boston in March 1776 also helped the independence movement. The declarations of independence by states and towns convinced even more delegates in Congress to publicly support independence.

On May 10, 1776, the Continental Congress unanimously approved the establishment of new colonial governments outside of British jurisdiction, a key step toward independence. On May 15, the Continental Congress just barely approved John Adams' preamble to the May 10 resolution. The preamble advised the colonial governments to denounce their allegiance to Britain and actively suppress British authority in America. Effectively, this was a declaration of war and independence.[62] John Adams wrote to his wife two days later, "Great Britain has at last driven America to the last step, a complete separation from her; a total, absolute independence, not only of her parliament, but of her crown. For such is the amount of the resolve of the 15th."[63]

Even at this late date, many still opposed independence. A number of states instructed their delegates to disapprove of any measure that did not work toward reconciliation.[64] As a result, four colonies voted against the preamble and a fifth abstained.

By July, the Continental Congress recognized that it had no choice but to declare independence. Even though Britain and America would try to reconcile their differences until at least 1778,[65] Congress realized that they would need foreign assistance to win the war but that no nation would help America if its objective was reconciliation.[66] Countries like France, Spain, or the Dutch Republic wanted to see Britain weakened. Reconciliation would have made Britain even stronger. Declaring independence was the only way to win the support of Britain's enemies.

By the time the Continental Congress declared independence in July 1776, thousands of Americans, dozens of towns, and a number of states had already done so.[67] The Declaration of Independence was just a final formality. The states had already established independent governments and the people were already fighting for their liberty. The Declaration of Independence merely expressed the sentiments that already existed across the colonies. Jefferson admitted this nearly 50 years later in a letter to Henry Lee:

> This was the object of the Declaration of Independence. Not to find out new principles, or new arguments, never before thought of, not merely to say things which had never been said before; but to place before mankind the common sense of the subject, in terms so plain and firm as to command their assent, and to justify ourselves in the independent stand we are compelled to take. Neither aiming at originality of principle or sentiment, nor yet copied from any particular and previous writing, it was intended to be an expression of the American mind, and to give to that expression the proper tone and spirit called for by the occasion. All its authority rests then on the harmonizing sentiments of the day, whether expressed in conversation, in letters, printed essays, or in the elementary books of public right, as Aristotle, Cicero, Locke, Sidney, &c.[68]

With Jefferson's Declaration of Independence, the cautious Founding Fathers caught up to the angry mobs that had been rebelling against Britain for years. Even with independence declared and the war progressing, the Founding Fathers approached the war thoughtfully and cautiously, not with the same enthusiasm and rebelliousness as the angry mobs.

WASHINGTON'S MILITARY STRATEGY

In many respects, the Continental Congress was a reactionary organization. They declared independence only after many others had already done so. Congress continued pushing for reconciliation long after the fighting had begun. They went to war only after it was already being fought.

Nevertheless, the Continental Congress's choice of George Washington to lead the new Continental Army was probably the key to winning the revolution and the war. After the war, Thomas Jefferson wrote about George Washington: "The moderation and virtue of a single character have probably prevented this Revolution from being closed, as most others have been, by a subversion of that liberty it was intended to establish."[69]

Congress gave George Washington a dubious task. Washington had to turn a group of farmers into a military force capable of beating the world's most powerful army. Washington explained in a letter to his brother, "I believe I may with great truth affirm, that no man perhaps since the first institution of armies ever commanded one under more difficult circumstances, than I have done."[70]

With his untrained and outnumbered army, Washington started off poorly. He retreated repeatedly from the British army. He lost both New York City and Philadelphia. Washington's popularity declined and there was even talk of replacing him as commander-in-chief.[71]

In retrospect, Washington's strategy of retreating, thereby saving the army to fight another day, was brilliant. Washington realized that his untrained and undisciplined army was no match for the British and that they would lose in open combat. Washington decided to use the vastness of America, not its people, against Britain. Britain had four times the population, a larger army, and a more powerful navy, but even Britain's navy and army could not control America's entire Atlantic coast and interior. Washington merely had to avoid direct conflict when the odds were against him. Washington could retreat from countless battles, fight and win small skirmishes such as the Battles of Trenton and Princeton, and train his army while waiting for the perfect opportunity to win a decisive battle. George Washington had to delay for more than five years before the opportunity presented itself at Yorktown in October 1781.

Washington's strategy was very much the opposite of that employed by the angry mobs. Instead of rushing into war full of passion, Washington took a thoughtful and cautious approach. Even as commander-in-chief of the Continental Army, Washington avoided violence as much as possible. Whereas the angry mobs loved action, Washington would have preferred tending his farm at Mount Vernon. In fact, he resigned from public service three times to do just that—after the

French and Indian War, after the War for Independence, and after serving two terms as President.

Washington's military brilliance was not in tactics or maneuvers, but in knowing when to fight and when to retreat. After the British evacuated Boston in March 1776, George Washington feared they would attack New York City. Washington took his army of under 20,000 men to Long Island, but the British army of 30,000 troops followed him.[72] Recognizing his disadvantage, Washington miraculously smuggled his army across the East River under the cover of fog, then escaped across the Hudson River into New Jersey, and fled from the British all the way to Pennsylvania. Disaffected American troops returned home and Washington's army dropped to just 3,000 men.[73] Defending his actions, Washington summarized his strategy in a report to Congress in September 1776: "We should on all Occasions avoid a general Action, or put anything to the Risque, unless compelled by a necessity, into which we ought never to be drawn."[74]

Washington did not have to wait long to prove his critics wrong. On Christmas night 1776, Washington and his army crossed the Delaware River to attack a Hessian camp at Trenton. An American defeat then and there might have meant the end of the revolution, but a victory would turn the course of the war. With the odds in their favor, Washington's army captured about 1,000 Hessian soldiers in a stunning military victory. Just a week later, Washington defeated the British army at Princeton.

George Washington never expected to defeat the entire British army in open warfare. In fact, Washington lost more battles than he won. However, Washington realized that he did not have to win a full war. He simply had to outlast the British. He needed to win a battle once in a while to lift American spirits and reduce British support for the war. Washington only had to wait long enough for the British to tire of expending their lives and fortunes.

Minor victories, such as those at Trenton and Princeton, were key to Washington's strategy. These victories silenced Washington's critics and the troops who abandoned the army returned. This ensured that the war would be long and drawn out, increasing the odds that Britain would grow tired of the war and give up without actually losing. By 1778, Britain was offering concessions to America and proposing a resumption of their prior relationship.[75] But it was too late. By this time, America was winning the war and would accept nothing less than complete independence.

Nevertheless, Britain was too stubborn to give up because, as Alexis de Tocqueville explains, "There are two things which will always be difficult for a democratic nation to do: beginning and ending a war."[76] Though Britain was not a democracy, King George III and Prime Minister Lord North still had to answer to the people. To retreat and admit defeat in 1778 would have hurt the power of the king and the current government. In fact, the king lost much of his power and Lord North's government fell after Britain lost the war just a few years later. Afraid of the political repercussions of retreating or admitting defeat, Britain continued fighting for many years.

CHAPTER THREE

THE WAR FOR INDEPENDENCE

Although the War for Independence was fought primarily between the thirteen colonies and Britain, the war was much larger and more complicated than that. Britain also fought against Spain, France, and the Dutch Republic. Britain was fighting in North America and all around the world. At the same time, Americans fought a civil war between those still loyal to Britain and those wanting independence, with an even larger number of neutrals caught in the crossfire. The Founding Fathers worked hard to protect all Americans, but the angry mobs were just as willing to attack Americans loyal to Britain or those who remained neutral as they were to fight the British army.

Even as the angry mobs and Founding Fathers disagreed with each other on many issues, they joined forces to battle the British together. With "the protection of Divine Providence,"[1] America emerged victorious. Nevertheless, this long war inflicted heavy damage on America and left the nation with an uncertain future.

AMERICAN PATRIOTISM

Although the angry mobs instigated the American Revolution with passion and enthusiasm, maintaining those emotions throughout the long and difficult years of war proved impossible. Furthermore, once the war was underway, it became evident that many Americans had no preference for or against independence and most who supported the revolution were unwilling to fight and die for it, especially when it looked like their cause was hopeless.

In reality, most Americans stayed home and worked their farms during the war. In 1776, the peak year for war mobilization, about 90,000 Americans fought in the revolution out of an eligible population of about 700,000.[2] Many of these enlistments were for just a few weeks or months, so the size of the military force at any one time was significantly lower. As the war lengthened, enthusiasm waned and enlistment dropped. Therefore, at most times, only a few percent of adult males fought for independence.

Furthermore, most of these men enlisted with state militias. These were often used only for defense, were not necessarily part of the effort to defeat the British army, and often did not even require the soldiers to leave home. Washington's Continental Army had at most 27,000 troops on paper and probably fewer than 17,000 in reality at its peak.[3] In contrast, Britain had 50,000 troops in North America, hired 30,000 Germans to fight for them, and devoted half its navy to the American War for Independence.[4]

After chasing George Washington and his army out of New York and through New Jersey in the summer and fall of 1776, the British army made camp in New Jersey. The British promised the citizens of New Jersey that they would protect their lives and property if they would swear allegiance to Britain. Thousands did. The New Jersey militia, which supposedly consisted of 17,000 troops, produced just 1,000 men to fight against the British.[5] Similarly, the size of Washington's army declined to just 3,000 troops.[6] The enthusiasm for the war had disappeared amid the fear of British harassment and following Washington's retreat from New York and New Jersey. Even if these Americans favored independence, they were not willing to risk their lives and property on what they increasingly saw as a hopeless cause. Patrick Henry's "Give Me Liberty or Give Me Death" sounded noble, but few were willing to put it into practice.

When Washington defeated the Hessians in the Battle of Trenton in December 1776 and the British in the Battle of Princeton in January 1777, many Americans switched back to the Patriot cause and rejoined the New Jersey militia and Washington's army. One Briton who was in America at the time described the change after the Battle of Trenton:

"The news is confirmed. The minds of the people are much altered. A few days ago they had given up the cause for lost. Their late successes have turned the scale and now they are all liberty mad again."[7]

Washington saw his army shrink again during the cold and wet winter of 1777-1778 at Valley Forge. Thousands of soldiers abandoned the cause and 2,500 died of starvation and disease.[8] Patriotism and enthusiasm could only take the army so far. The Continental Congress had no power to tax and, therefore, no means to provide for its army. Without an effective national government, the army could only beg for food and clothing. Many soldiers scavenged the countryside for food, stole from local farmers, or gave the farmers worthless paper money after taking their produce.

Patriotism was even lower in the South. By 1780, only 800 people were still fighting for the Southern Continental Army. At the same time, the British army picked up recruits by requiring men to join them or have their houses and crops burned. The South, which was always more Loyalist, had become solidly British.[9]

Britain controlled the South until the American victory at the Battle of Cowpens in January 1781. Nearly 2,000 American troops defeated a British force of approximately 1,100—killing more than 100 men, wounding about 200, and capturing in excess of 700. Chief Justice John Marshall explains: "Seldom has a battle in which greater numbers were not engaged, been so important in its consequences as that of the Cowpens. By it, Lord Cornwallis was not only deprived of a fifth of his numbers, but lost, so far as respected infantry, that active part of his army."[10] Although America took the advantage in the South with its victory at Cowpens, even this pivotal battle failed to boost American recruitment.[11]

Britain suffered from the same lack of enthusiasm. Forty-two thousand sailors deserted the British navy, but many of these sailors did not want to be there to start with because Britain conscripted one quarter or more of its 171,000 sailors.[12] Likewise, a number of Hessian soldiers deserted.[13]

The whole war was a battle of enthusiasm. For more than six years, the two sides fought back and forth with no end in sight. Minor victories, such as Trenton and Princeton, produced huge swings in sentiment even though they had limited military significance. Washington knew this before he crossed the Delaware River on that cold winter night. He knew that a victory would not end the war nor give America the military advantage. However, he knew that it would lift America's spirits, that many of the troops who had deserted would return, and that it would hurt British morale. In a war of ideas and passions, enthusiasm and perseverance are much more important than military capabilities or territorial control.

AMERICA'S FIRST CIVIL WAR

The idea that the War for Independence pitted all Americans against Britain is simplistic and incorrect. In fact, America was very much divided about independence and war. Prior to the spring of 1776, America was divided into four camps about equal in size: those loyal to Britain, those favoring independence, those favoring reconciliation, and those who were neutral.[14] As the war intensified, the group supporting reconciliation completely disappeared, but most from that camp would stay neutral throughout the war. Nevertheless, the number of people supporting independence increased as the war progressed while the number of Loyalists declined, many of them fleeing to Canada, other British colonies, or to Britain itself. In total, up to 100,000 Loyalists, about a fifth of the total, fled America during or immediately after the war to escape vengeance-seeking Patriots.[15]

Aiding the Patriots were a number of Canadians who came south to fight against the British.[16] However, many more Canadians fought against America when the Continental Army invaded Canada in 1775. Additionally, nearly 20,000 white Americans fought in the British army and thousands more fought in loyalist militias.[17] Much like the colonial militias, these militiamen were trying to protect the lives and property of their friends and neighbors.

The proportions of Patriots and Loyalists varied by ancestry and location. Scots were mostly Loyalist. Irish, Scots-Irish, and Huguenots were usually Patriots. English, Dutch, and Germans were neutral or just about evenly divided between the Patriot and Loyalist causes.[18] In some areas, such as New York, New Jersey, and Georgia, Loyalists likely outnumbered Patriots, though the neutrals outnumbered each of them and likely outnumbered the two opposing forces combined.[19] In the Loyalist stronghold of Queens, New York, for instance, 27 percent declared themselves Loyalist while only 12 percent declared themselves Patriot. That left about 60 percent neutral.[20]

Americans had a number of reasons to be Loyalist and not just because of a loyalty to Britain. Like many of the Founding Fathers, Loyalists feared the anarchy that comes with war. They feared that a war for independence would lead to "the horrors of civil war."[21] They also feared the tyranny of the majority that might come with an American victory, including the popular demand for redistribution of wealth.[22]

In contrast, the rebels believed that a civil war could be avoided only through independence. Thomas Paine wrote in *Common Sense*, "But the most powerful of all arguments, is, that nothing but independance, i.e. a continental form of government, can keep the peace of the continent and preserve it inviolate from civil wars." Paine added, "Independance is the only BOND that can tye and keep us together."[23] In hindsight, declaring independence did not prevent a civil war. Instead, it created one in the 1770s and led to an even greater civil war in the 1860s.

Despite the war, most Americans were neutral. Most neutrals were simply apolitical, not caring much whether they lived under a federal, state, or colonial government. Many stayed neutral for fear of reprisal from one side or the other or because they believed that the war was not worth the loss of life and expense. Most Americans simply wanted to live and work in peace, regardless of who was in power.

Lieutenant General William Howe, Commander-in-Chief of the British forces in America, described the many varying opinions of the American people: "Much might be said upon the state of loyalty, and the principles of loyalty, in America. Some are loyal from principle; many from interest; many from resentment; many wish for peace, but are indifferent which side prevails; and there are others who wish success to Great-Britain, from a recollection of the happiness they enjoyed under her government."[24]

With most Americans avoiding active participation in the war, it was not a battle of numbers or military strength. Instead, it was a war of enthusiasm and perseverance. The angry mobs provided an abundance of enthusiasm while Washington's military strategy and the Patriot's belief in the truth and inevitability of their cause provided the perseverance. In contrast, most Loyalists had little enthusiasm for British rule—they just did not want the chaos and uncertainty that came with war. The perseverance for the Loyalists would have to come from the British army and navy. However, the British eventually tired of spending their lives and fortune on a country almost none of them had visited.

In total, Americans did not form one cohesive group. There were Patriots and Loyalists, but the degree of their support varied considerably. There were also many neutrals who were apolitical, stayed neutral for fear of reprisal, or supported independence but not the war. Because of these divisions, the war between America and Britain was also a war between Americans, often between brothers or between fathers and sons. One Hessian colonel wrote, "Neighbors are on opposite sides, children are against their fathers."[25] For example, Benjamin Franklin's son William was the Royal Governor of New Jersey and a Loyalist who actively supported Britain during the war. Benjamin and William Franklin stopped communicating when the war started and the Patriots imprisoned William for his Loyalism. Benjamin and William Franklin never reconciled, even after the war ended.

With the number of Patriots and Loyalists nearly equal, the advantage in the War for Independence swung back and forth between the two sides. For instance, when the British chased Washington and his army through New York and New Jersey, the soldiers of the Continental Army and New Jersey militia deserted and rejoined the general population. New Jersey Patriots feared for their lives, the lives of their families, and their property when the Loyalists took power. When Washington defeated the British in the winter of 1776-1777, it was the Loyalists' turn to go into hiding in fear of the resurgent Patriots. Other states also swung back and forth, such as Georgia, which the Loyalists briefly controlled in 1779 before the British army headed north and the Patriots regained control.[26]

The Patriots and Loyalists often fought against each other with little or no British involvement. In South Carolina, a center of Loyalism, 103 of the 137 battles fought were between South Carolina Loyalists and South Carolina Patriots with few, if any, British soldiers involved.[27] One such battle was fought at King's Mountain on October 7, 1780. About one thousand American Patriots fought against an equally-sized pro-British army, composed primarily of American Loyalists commanded by a British officer. The battle was a resounding victory for the Patriots, who suffered few casualties, while the entire British and Loyalist contingent was killed, wounded, or captured. Many battles like this were fought across America during the war. However, the battles between the Continental and British armies receive most of the attention because they were often larger and more decisive. Nevertheless, these minor battles were important to the war because they influenced enthusiasm, affected enlistment in the army, and determined who controlled territories and their food supplies.

Both the Patriots and Loyalists mistreated their enemies and even innocent neutrals. Upon gaining control of an area, the conquering army often seized the produce and livestock of the farmers.[28] Both Patriots and Loyalists murdered innocents and attacked or imprisoned many who wished to remain neutral.[29] Major William Pierce, a future delegate to the Constitutional Convention, described the brutality of both sides in this war:

> Such scenes of desolation, bloodshed and deliberate mur-der I never was a witness to before! Wherever you turn the weeping widow and fatherless child pour out their melancholy tales to wound the feelings of humanity. The two opposite principles of whiggism and toryism have set the people of this country to cutting each other's throats, and scarce a day passes but some poor deluded tory is put to death at his door. For the want of civil government the bands of society are totally disunited, and the people, by copying the manners of the British, have become perfectly savage.[30]

Even those Patriots who defended accused Loyalists were often attacked by angry mobs. In October 1779, an angry mob attacked the home of James Wilson—brigadier general in the Pennsylvania State Militia, a signer of the Declaration of Independence, member of the Continental Congress, and later an influential and active delegate in the Constitutional Convention and one of the original six Supreme Court Justices. James Wilson had become "offensive" to the more radical revolutionaries after he defended merchants who violated price controls and two other men accused of being "tories and traitors." Following an investigation into the Fort Wilson Riot, the Pennsylvania House unanimously resolved "that this House will at all times support…the executive authority in suppressing all such dangerous and disorderly proceedings, and in restoring peace, good order, and a due obedience to government, on which the liberty, happiness, and safety of the citizens of the State so greatly depend."[31]

AMERICA'S LARGEST SLAVE REBELLION

As America waged war against Britain and Patriots battled Loyalists, slaves mounted the largest slave rebellion in American history and possibly the largest since Rome's Servile Wars. Gary Nash, author of *The Forgotten Fifth: African Americans in the Age of Revolution*, calls this "a revolution within a revolution."[32] It could also be called a civil war within a civil war.

The slave revolts began even before the War for Independence. Thomas Paine wrote in *Common Sense* that Britain "stirred up the Indians and Negroes to destroy us"[33] and Thomas Jefferson wrote in the Declaration of Independence that the King of Britain "has excited domestic insurrections amongst us." However, contrary to Jefferson and Paine, the slaves who fought for Britain did so of their own volition and volunteered even before Britain recruited them.[34] However, many blacks also fought for the Patriot side in the revolution.

Like white Americans, the black community was not a monolithic group that fought for just one side. Instead, blacks fought for whichever side offered them the greatest chance for freedom. In *The Negro in the American Revolution*, Benjamin Quarles explains, "The Negro's roles in the Revolution can best be understood by realizing that his major loyalty was not a place nor to a people, but to a principle. Insofar as he had freedom of choice, he was likely to join the side that made him the quickest and best offer in terms of those "unalienable rights" of which Mr. Jefferson had spoken. Whoever invoked the image of liberty, be he American or British, could count on a ready response from the blacks."[35]

Just like white colonists, blacks also divided their loyalty depending largely on each person's location and individual situation. In the North, where most African Americans were free and living relatively well, they sided with the Patriots to oppose Britain's attempts to reduce the liberties of all Americans. In fact, blacks in the North were twice as likely to fight for the Patriot cause as whites. At Bunker Hill, for instance, five percent of the American force was black, whereas just one to two percent of Massachusetts residents were black. Furthermore, in a show of patriotism by both black slaves and their owners in the North, many masters offered their slaves freedom if they would fight against Britain.[36] Thus, both free blacks and black slaves in the North fought for freedom by joining the Patriot cause.

In the South, though, most blacks fought for the British. More accurately, they fought against their owners. Slaves in Virginia started revolting against their masters in early 1775 and offered to fight for Britain a full six months before Lord Dunmore offered them freedom for their service. When Lord Dunmore made his offer to Virginia's slaves, thousands fled their masters to fight for Britain. Thousands more fled their masters to live free in the North or the West. Among the many slaves who fled their masters during the American Revolution were 20 belonging to George Washington and at least 23 owned by Thomas Jefferson.[37]

According to one estimate, 5,000 blacks served in the American army and navy but about 100,000 joined the British army.[38] Jefferson estimated that about 30,000 slaves from Virginia alone joined the British[39] while Gary Nash writes that "current research suggests" about 10,000 slaves from Virginia joined Britain.[40] Nevertheless, this slave rebellion certainly exceeded other famous American slave rebellions, such as Nat Turner's 1831 rebellion involving just a few dozen slaves and free blacks.[41]

Even at the very end of the war, slaves continued to flee their masters in a final effort to gain their freedom. Thousands of slaves fled to the

British side just prior to the Battle of Yorktown, sensing that this might be their last opportunity for freedom. Even after the Battle of Yorktown, several thousand slaves tried to flee, but their masters hired newly unemployed soldiers to capture the runaway slaves. Though the British lost the war, they did all they could to provide freedom to the slaves who joined them, even providing full compensation to their former masters.[42]

Even in the North, some black slaves joined the British to fight for their freedom and for the freedom of the slaves in the South. In Massachusetts, Abigail Adams wrote in September 1774 that the blacks drew "up a petition to the Governor, telling him they would fight for him provided he would arm them and engage to liberate them if he conquered."[43] In Pennsylvania, Henry Muhlenberg, a German Lutheran minister, reported that the slaves there "secretly wish that the British army might win, for then all Negro slaves will gain their freedom."[44]

Black participation in the American Revolution was all about liberty, even more than it was for white Americans. Sometimes that meant fighting with the Patriots against Britain, but more often it meant joining the British against Southern slaveholders. This was America's largest slave rebellion and was one of a few civil wars that occurred within the War for Independence.

PARTNERS IN WAR

The angry mobs started the revolution and even overthrew British colonial governments, but Britain continued oppressing America and the angry mobs could not restore law and order. Meanwhile, the Founding Fathers tried but failed to reconcile America's differences with Britain. Although the angry mobs and Founding Fathers disagreed on certain elements of the revolution, they still fought for the same goals. Only by working together were they able to win the War for Independence.

When the Continental Congress took control of the military and placed men like George Washington in charge of the war effort, they combined the power and enthusiasm of the angry mobs with the knowledge and experience of men, such as George Washington, who studied and experienced war.

In the summer of 1777, British General John Burgoyne led his army south from Canada to the Hudson Valley. The colonists blocked roads and destroyed bridges, slowing Burgoyne's army of 11,000 to a rate of just one mile a day. Burgoyne's primary concern became not one of winning a battle, but of supplying food for his troops. It also gave the Continental Army time to organize, enabling 10,000 troops led by Generals Horatio Gates and Benedict Arnold to defeat the British at Saratoga.

The Battle of Saratoga was a pivotal event in the war. This victory convinced France to recognize the United States and to provide military and financial support. Britain shifted its focus from New England and the Hudson Valley to the South to be closer to its possessions in the West Indies, which became vulnerable with France's entry into the war. Britain abandoned Philadelphia, concentrated its northern armies in New York and Rhode Island, shifted troops to the West Indies, and focused on capturing southern ports with the plan to then march northward with the support of Southern Loyalists.

Britain's chances of winning declined with France's entry into the war. Britain could no longer muster its full strength against America as British troops and ships in the West Indies were no longer available to fight the American rebels. To remedy its weakened state, British attacks became more brutal as Britain shelled American ports and raided the country-side. Britain also persuaded a number of rebel leaders to turn to the British side, most notably Benedict Arnold.

Britain offered to restore its relationship with America to that which existed before 1763.[45] However, fresh off a major military victory and with the French about to provide support to their cause, Americans saw no reason to end the war when independence appeared within reach. By 1778, when Britain made its peace offer, America no longer believed in the British mercantilist system nor the divine right of kings. Britain had many benefits to offer America, most notably protection of shipping throughout the Atlantic and Mediterranean, but America and Britain no longer agreed philosophically.

As Britain diverted much of its navy to the West Indies, American merchants used their ships to great effect. The Confederation and state governments had no ships with which to fight Britain's powerful navy, but American merchants had the third largest fleet in the world. With trade to Britain cut off and the domestic shipping business interrupted by British activities, most American ships and sailors were idle. America used its inactive merchant fleet to attack British shipping, devoting about 1,700 ships to privateering. This cost the British dearly and was very profitable for America. American privateers captured approximately 2,000 British ships and 12,000 sailors. Additionally, they captured about £18 million worth of goods, much of which the Americans took home with them, the rest of which was sunk or burned.[46]

Benjamin Franklin described the benefits of privateering: "While America is enriching itself by prizes made upon the British Commerce, more than ever it did by any Commerce of its own, under the Restraints of a British Monopoly, Britain is growing poorer by the loss of that Monopoly, the diminution of its revenues, and of course less able to discharge the present indiscreet Encrease of its Expences."[47] Franklin also remarked that capturing British ships and their crews "increase the Number of our Seamen, and thereby augment our naval Power."[48]

The fear of American privateers forced Britain to resort to convoys.[49] Britain used its navy to defend its merchant marine when the navy could have been attacking American coastal towns. France's entry into the war in early 1778 further distracted the British navy. Britain was forced to defend English coastal towns from French attack,[50] diverting resources away from the war in America. Spain entered the war in 1779 and the Dutch Republic in 1780. Britain was fighting three of the most powerful countries in Europe and the emerging American power, all at the same time. Britain was fighting on the American mainland and in the Atlantic, Caribbean, Mediterranean, Indian Ocean, North Sea, and English Channel.[51] With Britain increasingly distracted from the war in America by American privateers and new foreign enemies, the probabilities of a British victory declined.

Even with successful American privateering, the victory at Saratoga, and the entry of France, Spain, and the Dutch into the war, Britain was still the world's most powerful Empire. They had the world's most productive economy and strongest army and navy.

Britain shifted the war to the South, closer to its important colonies in the West Indies. Britain captured Savannah and Augusta in the winter of 1778-1779 and Charleston in May 1780. Meanwhile, George Washington was stuck in the North trying to keep his army together as soldiers mutinied. The American army suffered defeat after defeat and thousands of its soldiers surrendered to the British. America was on the brink of defeat yet again.

As the Continental Army lost to the well-trained and well-equipped British army, the British army and its Loyalist supporters took vengeance on the American rebels.[52] In response, individual Americans and local militias took up the cause. The Patriots harassed the British army as it moved north and regained control of most of the Southern states. Britain simply did not have the troops to conquer and control such a large country against determined resistance. Britain could conquer territory and hold it for a short time, but it could not conquer the American people.

OVERLY OPTIMISTIC EXPECTATIONS

Many Patriots expected the War for Independence to result in a quick victory. America knew that Britain had four times the number of people, was much wealthier, had the world's strongest army and navy, and had a manufacturing base from which to replenish supplies. However, the Patriots were counting on Britain's lag in communications, the time and expense of sending over troops and equipment from Britain, America's vast interior full of dense forests in which a disciplined army could not use its regular tactics, and British commitments throughout the rest of its empire.

Thomas Paine convinced himself and his thousands of readers that the war would be quick and relatively inexpensive. In *The Crisis Number 1*, written in December 1776, Paine argued, "A single successful battle next year will settle the whole. America could carry on a two years war by the confiscation of the property of disaffected persons."[53] The Battle of Yorktown did not occur for another five years and the Peace of Paris was nearly seven years away. The confiscation of the Loyalists' possessions would not have covered the expense of the war and, furthermore, America was wise to respect the Loyalists' property rights and establish the new nation as one of laws and rights, not of arbitrary rules and vengeance.

Even George Washington hoped for a short war when he first took command of the Continental Army in March 1776. Washington planned to destroy General Howe's army while it was encamped in Boston, which he thought would convince Britain to sue for peace.[54] A winter storm with heavy wind, snow, and hail halted Washington's plan. This Nor'easter was a blessing in disguise. When the British left Boston thirteen days later, Washington went into town and saw that his army would most likely have lost the battle. To his brother, Washington wrote, "Much blood was saved, and a very important blow, to one side or the other, was prevented. That this most remarkable interposition of Providence is for some wise purpose, I have not a doubt."[55] To Joseph Reed, Washington wrote about the British defenses in Boston: "Their works all standing, upon examination of which, especially at Bunker's Hill, we find amazingly strong: twenty thousand men could not have carried it against one thousand, had that work been well defended. The town of Boston was almost impregnable—every avenue fortified."[56]

Washington and the Patriots had underestimated the British defenses and overestimated their chances of a quick victory. Even if General Washington's plan succeeded, though he admitted it likely would have failed, it would not have brought the quick victory America had hoped for and expected. Washington and America did not know that an army four times the size of the one in Boston was already heading over from Britain.[57]

In the summer of 1776, Washington requested 40,000 soldiers for the duration of the war. Seeing the apparent success of part-time militiamen against the British at Lexington, Concord, Bunker Hill, and Ticonderoga, Congress granted Washington only 20,000 men for one year,[58] but Congress had difficulty paying for an army even that small. When Washington arrived in New York City that summer with 20,000 men— 10,000 men in his army and another 10,000 or so in the militia—they faced a British army in excess of 30,000 troops, more than the entire population of Philadelphia, the largest city in the thirteen colonies. Washington and his army barely escaped from Brooklyn and then Manhattan. In fact, their escape from Brooklyn was only made possible when wind prevented Britain's fleet from entering the East River and fog enabled the colonists to flee in secret to Manhattan.

A MIRACULOUS VICTORY

America was fortunate to find itself fighting Britain in 1776 instead of 1763. After the Seven Years War ended in 1763, the threat from the recently defeated French was greatly reduced. Additionally, Britain amassed a huge debt fighting that war and had large interest payments to make. No longer fearing the French and needing to cut spending, Britain reduced the strength of its army and navy, boosting America's chances in the war between them.

Nevertheless, the American victory over Britain in the War for Independence was not inevitable. In fact, a number of Founding Fathers considered America's success in the war to be a miracle. George Washington wrote in March 1781, "We have, as you very justly observe, abundant reasons to thank Providence for its many favorable interpositions in our behalf. It has at times been my only dependence, for all other resources seemed to have failed us."[59]

In *What If?: The World's Foremost Military Historians Imagine What Might Have Been*, Thomas Fleming writes about "Thirteen Ways the Americans Could Have Lost the Revolution." Robert Cowley, editor of the *What If?* series, summarizes: "By any reasonable stretch of the imagination, Fleming reminds us, the United States should have expired at birth. We were hardly inevitable."[60] The thirteen ways America could have lost include the storm that hit Boston in March 1776 that stopped George Washington from attacking the British with likely disastrous results and the escape of Washington and his army from Brooklyn in August 1776 protected by the wind and under the cover of fog.

The victories at Trenton and Princeton in the winter of 1776-1777 are also listed among the miracles. Crossing the Delaware River in the middle of winter was a risky proposition. Again, favorable weather conditions enabled the army to cross the river but lulled the British and Hessians into a false sense of security. Additionally, the British and Hessians did not expect the American army to attack in the middle of winter when most armies set up their winter encampments and avoid battles. The password of "Victory or Death" aptly described the situation. If the weather had turned against Washington, the Continental Army could have been lost without the British firing a shot. If Washington had been captured or killed by the Hessians or British or if a large portion of his army been lost, it is difficult to see how America could have continued to fight with its leader gone or the bulk of its army captured or killed.

In December 1777, more than 10,000 American troops entered Valley Forge for the winter. In the next few months, 2,500 Americans died of starvation, freezing cold, and illness because of a lack of food, clothing, and blankets. Thousands more deserted or pillaged the countryside to provide for their needs. While the Continental Army encamped at Valley Forge, General Howe and his army of about 14,000 troops were just twenty miles away in Philadelphia. They too had some difficulty obtaining food and clothing, but they had secure lodging and were much better off than the Continental Army. Nobody knows for certain why General Howe chose not to attack Washington and his army. It is possible that General Howe did not know just how dire the situation was at Valley Forge and how easy a victory could have been. Alternatively, maybe he did know and preferred letting the cold winter and inadequate supplies fight his war for him. Many, though, attribute Howe's inaction to his overly cautious attitude. Choosing not to press his advantage, as Washington had done a year earlier at Trenton and Princeton, might have cost General Howe a major victory in the war and the capture or killing of Washington and his army.

Yet another weather event was key to the American victory in the War for Independence. In the autumn of 1781, a large portion of the British army found itself at Yorktown, Virginia. After a three-week siege by American troops and the French fleet, General Cornwallis and his army surrendered. The war was over, for all intents and purposes.

If not for the weather, the British army might have won that battle or escaped to fight another day. Just days before the final battle at Yorktown, a fleet of British ships was to set sail from New York City to the Chesapeake to assist the besieged British army. Suddenly, a thunderstorm struck and damaged some ships. The British decided to repair the damaged ships before setting sail. Back in Yorktown, the British army was retreating across the York River when another violent storm struck and the surging river blocked their retreat. Rather than face certain defeat in battle with thousands of casualties, the British surrendered.[61]

This was much more a British defeat than it was an American victory. At Yorktown, there were about 9,000 French troops and 8,000 American troops against 9,000 British and German troops. If the French had not been there, Britain likely would have fought the battle and possibly emerged victorious, though the Americans probably would not have even attacked in that situation.

Furthermore, the Battle of Yorktown was only decisive in retrospect. At the time, neither side knew that the war had ended. As Ray Raphael writes in *Founding Myths: Stories That Hide Our Patriotic Past*: "In the wake of Yorktown, George Washington insisted that the war was not yet over, and King George III was not ready to capitulate. In fact, the fighting continued for over a year."[62]

Back in 1777, more than 6,000 British troops surrendered at Saratoga. In fact, more troops were killed and wounded at Saratoga than at Yorktown. Nevertheless, after the British defeat at Saratoga, Britain continued fighting for another four years. Even with the surrender of nearly 8,000 British troops at Yorktown, Britain still had 30,000 soldiers in the thirteen colonies and another 10,000 in Canada. Though it lost the port of Yorktown, it still held the much more important ports of New York City, Savannah, and Charleston, in addition to Halifax in Canada and St. Augustine in Florida.[63]

In reality, Yorktown was not *the* decisive battle, but one of many battles that pushed Britain out of the war. Britain also lost battles in India, Florida, the West Indies, Minorca, and in the Atlantic. At the same time, the French and Spanish were threatening British control of the English Channel. Simply, Britain could not fight all these wars concurrently. Britain had to cut its losses if it were to avoid total defeat around the world. Furthermore, British debts had already risen too high to fund all these wars and the British people had grown tired of paying for the war with their money and their lives. The political support for the war had disappeared.

Britain decided to abandon its war in North America. Britain recognized that it could defeat the American army and even level most major cities, but it could not control the rebels, who would continue to fight as they had been doing for a decade. Britain also saw that America, being a world away and not interested in European politics, would become a neutral party in world affairs. The loss of America would be less significant than the loss of Gibraltar, which controls the narrow strait connecting the Mediterranean and Atlantic. In terms of Britain's naval power, possessing Gibraltar was much more important than America.

Britain also realized that it would still have the most beneficial trade status with America because they shared a common language, had similar cultures, and already had established business relations. Therefore, the economic cost of losing the United States would be much smaller than the military cost of losing Gibraltar or other key possessions. In the end, Britain lost the thirteen colonies, Minorca, and East and West Florida but kept Gibraltar, India, and the West Indies. Britain sacrificed its American colonies and other possessions to keep its even more valuable holdings.

Britain signed the Treaty of Paris with the United States in 1783, but also signed peace treaties with France and Spain that same year and a treaty with the Dutch Republic in the following year, demonstrating that Britain was interested in ending all its wars, not just the one with America. The British people had grown tired of war and British finances had deteriorated because of Britain's significant commitments around the world. Keeping only its most important possessions, Britain remained the strongest nation in the world.

Richard Oswald, the British envoy who negotiated the Treaty of Paris, told Benjamin Franklin "that the peace was absolutely necessary for them; that the nation had been foolishly involved in four wars, and would no longer be able to earn money to carry them on, so that if they continued, it would be absolutely necessary for them to stop payment of the interest money in the funds, which could ruin their future credit."[64]

America did not win the War for Independence through superior military or naval power, though it performed admirably against the British. Instead, America won the war because it outlasted the British, as was George Washington's strategy. America also received much needed financial and military help from Britain's enemies, without whose assistance America's victory would have been nearly impossible.

From the start, America was the underdog in this war. British land and naval forces outnumbered America's. American military leaders were poorly trained by British standards. George Washington had never commanded a large military force and had only fought in the wilderness. America had to hire Europeans such as Baron von Steuben to train the Continental Army. Even decades later when the population and economy of the United States had grown substantially, both nominally and relative to Britain, America lost the early stages of the War of 1812 to the British army and navy. An American victory in the War for Independence was far from inevitable.

Certainly, the war was not quick and inexpensive as Thomas Paine had written it would be or as George Washington had hoped. The angry mobs started the revolution against Britain under false pretenses and many were quick to give up the fight. Much to their credit, though, after hiding out for a while, the Patriots always reappeared when needed. By working together, along with help from France, Spain, the Dutch, and "Providence," the angry mobs and Founding Fathers miraculously defeated Britain and won their independence.

A COSTLY VICTORY

War is always costly, both in economic and human terms. This was one reason the Founding Fathers wished to avoid war with Britain. Twenty-five thousand Americans died in the War for Independence, about one percent of the nation's population. A much larger number had their homes destroyed and their livelihoods taken from them. Although only a small percentage of the population fought or died in the war, virtually everybody was negatively affected by it.

Certain areas, though, were more affected than others. The British occupied New York City for more than seven years, from 1776 to 1783. Half of the city's buildings were destroyed and the city's population was also halved. Many of those who remained in the city during the war were

Loyalists or neutrals who did business with the British during the war. Many of them left with the British in 1783 for fear of reprisal by the Patriots.[65]

In terms of population, the War for Independence had little or no effect on America. Although 25,000 men were killed in the war and up to 100,000 Loyalists fled America during and after the war, the population still grew by more than 600,000 in the 1770s and by more than 1,100,000 in the 1780s.[66] In total, population growth was slightly below average in the 1770s at 29.4 percent but rebounded to an above average 41.3 percent increase in the 1780s. The 35.4 percent population growth per decade during these two decades was nearly identical to the 36.0 percent growth rate per decade posted between 1700 and 1770 and the 35.4 percent growth rate per decade from 1780 to 1860.[67] Therefore, in terms of population, the war had little effect on the country. If it had any effect at all, it was only temporary.

After the war ended, America quickly returned to normal. Although the Loyalists were attacked and persecuted during the war, just as the Loyalists and British did to the Patriots, there were relatively few reprisals afterward and much of their seized property was returned to them.

Although there were few physical acts of vengeance on Loyalists after the war, some states wanted to punish them financially. New York passed a number of acts during and immediately after the war to protect Patriots and punish Loyalists. The Confiscation Act of 1779 allowed the state to take the property of any Loyalist, the Citation Act of 1782 shielded Patriots from Loyalist creditors, and the Trespass Act of 1783 enabled New Yorkers to sue Loyalists for damages done to their property even when authorized by the British government.[68] Alexander Hamilton made a specialty of defending these Loyalists in court. In addition to earning a living, Hamilton wanted to protect the property rights of all Americans and worried that prosecuting and persecuting wealthy Loyalists and neutrals would motivate them to move to Britain or Canada, where they would compete with New York and the United States.[69] In contrast, a strong defense of individual liberty and property rights would make New York and the United States an attractive place to do business. Though the civil war between the Patriots and Loyalists had ended, the political war between the angry mobs who wanted revenge and those who wished to maintain property rights continued.

The War for Independence imposed significant economic costs on America. International trade disappeared during the war and it took years to recover. Foreign trade accounted for 15 to 20 percent of output just prior to the revolution, but only recovered to 10 to 15 percent of output by the 1790s. Imports from Britain recovered quite quickly, but exports took decades to do so. However, America was now able to trade with other nations, most notably those in Northern Europe and the non-British West Indies. Much of America's exports went to these new trading partners. Britain's share of American exports declined from 58 percent prior to the war to 31 percent in the early 1790s.[70]

In total, between 1770 and 1790, American exports rose about 30 percent. However, the population grew by 83 percent in those twenty years. Thus, per capita exports fell by nearly a third. This reduced total per capita income by about five percent.[71]

Offsetting some of these losses, the prices received for exports rose as American goods no longer needed to go through Britain. At the same time, import prices declined as foreign goods and ships competed with Britain's.[72] As a result, America's trade deficit narrowed and the people's purchasing power rose. However, not all areas were affected evenly. While the North did fairly well, exports fell dramatically in the South,[73] in part because of the lost production of thousands of slaves who fled their masters during the war.

On top of this, America ran up a huge debt fighting the War for Independence. In 1791, after the United States assumed the war debts of the states and added it to its own, the national debt amounted to $75 million, almost 40 percent of gross domestic product. Consequently, many of the political battles in the 1780s and early 1790s concerned the financial situation of the nation—a lingering cost of the War for Independence.

In total, agricultural production declined during the war, domestic and international trade dropped, and foreign credit disappeared.[74] Years of potential economic growth were lost. The steady improvement in standards of living slowed and may have even fallen because of the war.[75]

Though the War for Independence cost many American lives and much money, as all wars do, it was a relatively cheap war. Henry Steele Commager and Richard B. Morris explain in *The Spirit of 'Seventy-Six: The Story of the American Revolution as Told by Participants*:

> The American Revolution was costly in lives and in property, and more costly in the terror and the fear and the violence that, as in all wars, fell so disproportionately on the innocent and the weak. Yet by comparison with other wars of comparable ruthlessness and even the ferocity with which it was waged, it did little lasting damage, and left few lasting scars. Population increased all through the war; the movement into the West was scarcely interrupted; and within a few years of peace, the new nation was bursting with prosperity and buoyant with hope.[76]

Nevertheless, the costs of the War for Independence were not just confined to the war period. After the war, Americans regretted losing the benefits that came with the colonial system, whereas the advantages of independence were not yet readily apparent.[77] Without British administration and protection, America would struggle under the inadequacies of its new government.

CHAPTER FOUR

CHAOS IN THE CONFEDERATION

A merica won its independence with the victory at the Battle of Yorktown in October 1781 and the Treaty of Paris in September 1783. A nation largely descended from outcasts and refugees proved to themselves and to the world that mercantilism, colonialism, and monarchism could be resisted and defeated. But the battle for America had just begun.

After winning its independence, America had before it the equally difficult task of keeping it. As Samuel Adams wrote after the war: "I thank God that I have lived to see my country independent and free. She may long enjoy her independence and freedom if she will. It depends on her virtue. She has gained the glorious prize, and it is my most fervent wish (in which I doubt not you heartily join me) that she may value and improve it as she ought."[1]

America's independence and freedom depended on the creation of new political institutions to replace those that were overthrown. The thirteen states wrote the Articles of Confederation in November 1777 to create a "perpetual Union between the States" and a "firm league of friendship with each other, for their common defense, the security of their liberties, and their mutual and general welfare, binding themselves to assist each other, against all force offered to, or attacks made upon them, or any of them."[2] Although these Articles were not officially ratified and put in force until March 1781, delayed by arguments over conflicting territorial claims in the West, Congress and the states operated under them in practice if not in law since their creation in 1777. Americans soon discovered that this system of Confederation had serious flaws that threatened the very rights and liberties they fought so hard to secure.

A WEAK AND INEFFECTIVE GOVERNMENT

The Confederation was a weak alliance of the states that gave Congress much responsibility but little power. Alexander Hamilton wrote about the Confederation: "It is certainly pernicious to leave any government in a situation of responsibility disproportioned to its power."[3] As a result, the period under the Confederation government was anarchic and chaotic. In fact, the weak national government put the entire revolution at risk.

The primary flaw of the Articles of Confederation was that the people did not see themselves as Americans, but rather as residents of their own states. The states guarded their powers jealously and acted slowly in setting up this Confederation. The Second Continental Congress took over a year to draft the Articles of Confederation and the states took four years to ratify it.[4]

The resulting federal government was extremely weak. The Articles of Confederation provided for no executive or judiciary. Congress could pass laws, but had no power to enforce them. In effect, Congress was just a committee that made recommendations for the states to follow or ignore.[5] Congress also lacked the power to tax but had the power to borrow and print money, and it did both recklessly to fund the war. Congress did request money from the states, as it was supposed to, but the states struggled to pay their own militias and the interest on their debts. As a result, the states were slow to fund the Confederation government. When the Confederation government tried to impose a five percent tax on imports, a move that required the unanimous consent of all thirteen states, some opposed the tax and blocked it, most notably New York.[6] As a result, Congress received just six percent of its funds from taxes during the War for Independence.[7] Consequently, the American Revolution was fought largely with worthless paper money and by borrowing from Britain's enemies.

The people's hatred of taxes, which in part launched the revolution, made it more difficult to field an army and defeat the British. When General George Washington requested 40,000 troops in 1776 for the duration of the war, Congress gave him just 20,000 for one year. In fact, Washington never even had that many because Congress lacked the funds to pay the soldiers. Congress was also unable to provide proper food and clothing, which had disastrous consequences, especially at Valley Forge. These Patriots, who joined the army to fight the British and protect their lives, liberty, and property, often had no choice but to steal from their fellow citizens just to survive.[8]

The Founding Fathers argued that Congress needed more power, including the power to tax. Sounding much like the British had after the French and Indian War, Benjamin Franklin complained that Americans were unwilling to pay taxes for their own defense: "Our people certainly ought to do more for themselves. It is absurd, this pretending to be lovers of liberty while they grudge paying for the defence of it. It is said here, that an impost of five per cent on all goods imported, though a most reasonable proposition, had not been agreed to by all the States, and was therefore frustrated; and that your newspapers acquaint the world with this, with the non-payment of taxes by the people, and with the non-payment of interest to the creditors of the public."[9]

When the war ended, most Americans turned their attentions to the economy and their individual livelihoods. Although the post-war economy recovered as soldiers returned to work, international trade resumed, and optimism abounded, the huge debts incurred to fight the war, the weaknesses of the Confederation government, and the devastation in the South, where most of the fighting occurred in the later years of the war, impeded economic growth.

Government finances were in a desperate situation. Interest on the war debt in 1785 amounted to about $3 million per year while the Confederation government took in revenue of less than $1 million each year.[10] Consequently, the Confederation government's debt continued to rise after the war as interest accrued. As a result, the United States defaulted on its debts.[11]

Unable to levy taxes without the unanimous consent of the states, Congress considered coercing the states into paying the funds requested from them. James Madison argued in 1781, "The necessity of arming Congress with coercive powers arises from the shameful deficiency of some of the States which are most capable of yielding their apportioned supplies, and the military exactions to which others, already exhausted by the enemy and our own troops, are in consequence exposed. Without such powers, too, in the General Government, the whole confederacy may be insulted, and the most salutary measures frustrated, by the most inconsiderable State in the Union."[12] Coercion was too extreme for Congress, so it tried again to pass a tax. Twelve of the thirteen states approved the new tax, but Rhode Island rejected it, denying Congress the unanimous consent needed for its enactment into law.[13] Congress remained powerless to tax, the treasury remained empty, and American credit nonexistent.

Lacking the power to tax and already borrowing to its limit, the Confederation government printed the money it needed. Just as money printing failed to ameliorate the gold and silver shortage during the colonial period, the Confederation's printing presses also created economic troubles for the new nation. Though the colonists blamed Britain for the money problems during the colonial period, the monetary system was even worse under the Confederation government.[14]

Starting in 1775, Congress printed paper money redeemable for gold or silver. Congress kept on printing as the cost of the war rose. As a result, the Continental Dollar had lost 33 percent of its value by early 1777. By late 1778, it had lost 90 percent of its value. By 1781, the Continental Dollar had lost more than 99 percent of its value and one silver dollar was worth 146 Continental Dollars.[15] In 1779, General George Washington asked Congress, "Is there any thing doing, or that can be done, to restore the credit of our money? The depreciation of it has got to so alarming a point, that a wagon-load of money will scarcely purchase a wagon-load of provisions."[16]

In Federalist No. 44, James Madison explained the far-reaching effects of all this paper money: "The loss which America has sustained since the peace, from the pestilent effects of paper money on the necessary confidence between man and man, on the necessary confidence in the public councils, on the industry and morals of the people, and on the character of republican government, constitutes an enormous debt against the States chargeable with this unadvised measure, which must long remain unsatisfied."

Despite the money problems, international trade recovered quickly after its nearly complete stoppage during the war. British merchants, many of whom opposed the war against America because of the business they would lose, worked hard to restore trade with their former colonies. They extended credit to American businesses and utilized their previous contacts and knowledge of the American market to gain the advantage over France and other nations. The British government even granted the United States some of the same benefits it extended to its own colonies.[17] As a result, Britain remained America's largest trading partner, though its share of America's exports and imports still declined.[18]

Within a few years, exports fully recovered to their pre-war levels.[19] However, exports per capita and as a percentage of economic output were still far below those earlier levels.[20] The trade benefits America expected from independence had not appeared. At the same time, some of the disadvantages of independence became quite obvious. The loss of British protection on the high seas damaged America's international commercial interests. Without British protection, Barbary pirates from North Africa seized American ships and sold the crews into slavery. The pirates demanded tribute and ransom, but Congress had no money to pay them and could not afford to wage war against them.[21]

Despite the limited recovery in foreign trade, depression followed the war as the prices of goods fell.[22] It was not just America that suffered. Britain, France, and Spain all incurred debt to fight their wars in the 1770s and had to cut back on spending in the 1780s. This global depression impeded foreign trade and deepened the effects of America's depression. Productivity declined and real wages fell by up to forty percent for some Americans.[23] James Madison described the situation in 1785: "In every point of view indeed the trade of this Country is in a deplorable Condition." Madison also pointed out that the condition in the South was much worse than in the North: "A comparison of current prices here with those in the Northern States, either at this time or at any time since the peace, will shew that the loss direct on our produce & indirect on our imports is not less than 50 per ct."[24]

Some had ideas to solve America's economic problems, but the state governments blocked them. In 1779, the 24-year-old Alexander Hamilton wrote to Robert Morris recommending a national bank. Over the next two years, Hamilton further developed his bank idea and corresponded with Morris.[25] Robert Morris was a wealthy financier and one of just two men to sign the Declaration of Independence, Articles of Confederation, and Constitution. When Morris became Superintendent of Finance in 1781, he immediately proposed a national bank to strengthen the currency and finance the debt. The Bank of North America was chartered on the last day of 1781 and opened in January 1782, but had limited success as the states jealously guarded their power to charter banks and restricted the actions of this national bank. Robert Morris also wanted to nationalize the war debt to strengthen the Union,[26] but the states did the opposite by converting nearly one third of the federal debt into state bonds.[27] This further weakened the national government because it made the owners of the debt beholden to the states.

The Confederation government was not without some success during its brief administration. The Northwest Ordinance of 1787 created a new territory east of the Appalachians and north of the Ohio River, established its government, guaranteed civil rights in the region, prohibited slavery in the new land, and even resolved some conflicting territorial claims.

The Confederation government also signed treaties with the Indians. However, the Confederation was too weak to enforce these agreements. The states and frontier settlers simply ignored the treaties and the Indians formed their own confederations to oppose America's westward expansion. The Indians and settlers fought repeatedly and the Confederation government was powerless to stop it.[28]

In *Democracy in America*, Alexis de Tocqueville summarizes the weaknesses of the government under the Articles of Confederation: "The federal government, condemned to weakness by its very constitution, and no longer sustained by the feeling of public danger, witnessed the outrages done to its flag by the great nations of Europe while it was unable to drum up sufficient resources to confront the Indian tribes or pay the interest on debts incurred during the War of Independence."[29]

CONSPIRACY, MUTINY, AND REBELLION

The angry mobs that fought against the British and Loyalists during the War for Independence did not just disappear after America's victory.

Many of the same people, along with new additions, were angered by the attempts of the Confederation and state governments to raise taxes, their inability to pay the army and militia veterans, the rampant inflation, and the lack of gold, silver, and credit. Just as the angry mobs protested and rebelled against British rule, they did the same against their own states and nation after the war ended.

Whereas the rebellion against British oppression was considered noble, the same actions against their own governments were seen in a different light. After the experiences of the pre-war protests, the civil wars during the War for Independence, and these new rebellions against their own governments, the general population realized that limits had to be placed on democracy to ensure law, order, peace, and prosperity.

Throughout the War for Independence, Congress failed to provide food and clothing to the army and was remiss in paying the soldiers. In 1780, Alexander Hamilton wrote, "It is now a mob, rather than an army; without clothing, without pay, without provision, without morals, without discipline. We begin to hate the country for its neglect of us. The country begin to hate us for our oppressions of them. Congress have long been jealous of us. We have now lost all confidence in them, and give the worst construction to all they do. Held together by the slenderest of ties, we are ripening for a dissolution."[30]

Years later, still upset they had not been paid, army officers circulated letters saying that the army would not disband until they were paid and that the army would refuse to protect Congress if attacked. Some even threatened to revolt against Congress and establish a constitutional monarchy. Delegates to Congress worried about a coup and suggested that George Washington meet with the officers from the army. In March 1783, Washington assembled the army officers in Newburgh, New York, and pledged to do all he could to help them but urged them to be patient. Seeing that the officers were unmoved by his arguments, Washington took out his glasses to read them a letter and remarked, "Gentlemen, you will permit me to put on my spectacles, for I have not only grown gray, but almost blind in the service of my country."[31] Upon hearing these words and recognizing the sacrifice General Washington made for his country and fellow Americans, many officers were brought to tears and the Newburgh Conspiracy evaporated.

Had George Washington failed to suppress the coup, it could have led to civil war. As Major General Nathanael Greene wrote about the potential coup: "When soldiers advance without authority, who can halt them?"[32] Angry mobs of soldiers demanding their pay would march on Congress. Merchants and farmers would form their own angry mobs to oppose higher taxes, just as they had done leading up to the revolution. The state governments would try to resist both groups. With a simple gesture and a few well-spoken words, George Washington put down an angry mob of army officers threatening another rebellion and prevented a potential civil war.

Meanwhile, the British still had an army and fleet in New York City at the time of the Newburgh Conspiracy. The British could have used a civil war to renew its war against America. Or the British could have waited and let the Americans weaken themselves before deciding whether to attack. Either way, though the fighting with Britain had ended, the threat of renewed war remained until the United States put itself on a much more solid footing.

With the successful appeasement of the Newburgh conspirators, George Washington won the peace just as he had won the war. King George III called Washington "the greatest man in the world" for refusing the monarchy that some of the conspirators offered him.[33] Washington's admirers nicknamed him Cincinnatus, after the Roman farmer and general who was made dictator on two different occasions to fight Rome's enemies and both times relinquished power after succeeding in his mission.

The Pennsylvania Mutiny of June 1783 followed right on the heels of the Newburgh Conspiracy. An angry mob of soldiers from the Continental Army marched toward Philadelphia to demand the back pay owed to them. Congress was powerless to stop them and lacked the money to pay them. They asked Pennsylvania Governor John Dickinson to call in the militia and stop the mob, but he resisted. Congress escaped from Philadelphia to New Jersey. Only after Congress escaped did Dickinson call in the militia and the mob dispersed. Congress did not return to Philadelphia until 1790, meeting instead in Princeton, then Annapolis, followed by Trenton, and finally in New York City.

The threat from the army largely disappeared when Congress finally paid the soldiers and disbanded the army following the signing of a peace treaty with Britain in September 1783. However, the Confederation government paid the soldiers with bonds whose values declined along with the government's financial situation. As a result, even after being paid, many soldiers were still upset with the government and participated in or led other rebellions.

Daniel Shays was one such army veteran disappointed by how the government treated veterans. Shays, who returned to farming after the war, was also angered by how creditors treated farmers who had borrowed money. As delegates from five states met in Annapolis in 1786 to try to fix some of the defects of the Articles of Confederation, Daniel Shays led a rebellion of 1,200 men against the Massachusetts government.

General Henry Knox wrote to George Washington explaining the objectives of Shays and his followers: "Their creed is, that the property of the United States has been protected from the confiscation of Britain by the joint exertions of all, and therefore ought to be the common property of all; and he that attempts opposition to this creed, is an enemy to equity and justice, and ought to be swept off the face of the earth... They are determined to annihilate all debts, public and private, and have agrarian laws, which are easily effected by the means of unfunded paper money, which shall be a tender in all cases whatever."[34]

Shays' Rebellion was put down in January 1787 by a well-armed force of 4,400 men. Alexander Hamilton noted how close America came to civil war: "Who can determine what might have been the issue of her late convulsions, if the malcontents had been headed by a Caesar or by a Cromwell?"[35]

The rebels were pardoned and they succeeded in elections the following year. The new legislature passed the debt relief that the rebels demanded.[36] The rebellion and the rebels' subsequent electoral success forced many people and government officials to recognize that the political system needed fixing.[37] All the states were scared into action because Shays' Rebellion occurred in the state thought to have the best constitution.[38]

The desire for a constitutional convention to repair the defects of the Articles of Confederation was growing. Whereas only five states attended the Annapolis Convention of September 1786, delegates from all thirteen states attended the Philadelphia Convention the following year.

THE TYRANNY OF THE STATES

After rebelling against the British government and its strong executive, the American colonies established governments at the other extreme. Upon declaring their independence, the states established governments that were far too democratic. They increased the number of representatives in their legislatures and the people elected less educated men. Pennsylvania created a government with only one house and no governor. Eight states moved their capitals from the coastline, where the merchants and wealthy lived, to more interior locations to be closer to the average citizen, most of whom were farmers.[39]

While these democratic adjustments made the government more responsive to the people's needs and desires, the government also became less capable and more prone to errors of judgment and emotion. In *The American Revolution: A History*, Gordon Wood explains, "All of these neoclassical dreams were soon overwhelmed by the egalitarian democracy that resulted from the Americans' grand experiment in republicanism."[40]

Because of the way the country developed, America had always been very democratic. Alexis de Tocqueville explains, "In America we can state that the organization of the township preceded that of the county, the county that of the state, the state that of the union... The towns appointed every rank of magistrate; levied and apportioned their own taxes. In the New England town, the law of representation had no place; the affairs which affected everyone were discussed, as in Athens, in the public squares or in the general assembly of the citizens."[41]

The rebellion against Britain reinforced this desire for democracy. However, the states quickly recognized their lack of and need for checks and balances. From 1777 through the 1790s, the states revised the constitutions that they created upon declaring independence. They strengthened their governors and judicial branches, made them more independent, created senates in states that lacked them, lengthened senatorial terms of service, raised the property requirement for membership in the senate, and weakened the popularly elected houses by reducing their size and authority.[42]

Alexis de Tocqueville explains the change in one of the most democratic states: "Only Pennsylvania, of all the united republics, had initially attempted to establish a single assembly. Franklin himself, attracted by the logical conclusions of the dogma of the sovereignty of the people, had agreed to this measure but they were soon forced to change the law and establish the two houses. Thus the principle of the division of the legislature received its final consecration."[43]

James Madison argued that no quantity of checks and balances could prevent the states from being too democratic because the individual states were small enough for factions to gain complete power. Madison wrote, "The smaller the society, the fewer probably will be the distinct parties and interests composing it; the fewer the distinct parties and interests, the more frequently will a majority be found of the same party; and the smaller the number of individuals composing a majority, and the smaller the compass within which they are placed, the more easily will they concert and execute their plans of oppression."[44]

The tyranny of the states often reflected and accompanied the tyranny of the angry mobs. In fact, the tyranny of the angry mobs often began where that of the state ended. What the states could not accomplish was done by angry mobs, including penalizing profiteers, enforcing price controls, and punishing Tories.[45] This was the case with the Fort Wilson Riot of October 1779, in which an angry mob attacked James Wilson's house after he defended accused Tories, alleged traitors, and violators of price controls.

Perhaps the biggest problem under the Articles of Confederation was in commerce. Without the uniform tariffs that Britain instituted and which the angry mobs rebelled against, each state determined its own tariffs. Initially, the states enacted tariffs on imports for the sole purpose of raising revenue, but gradually the states made protectionism a secondary objective.[46] Each state imposed steep tariffs on foreign imports of certain goods to protect that state's businesses and workers. This created a hodgepodge of tariffs, which shippers avoided by importing the enumerated goods into low-tax ports and reshipping them tax free to other ports. And while most states did not impose tariffs on each other,[47] Connecticut did impose higher taxes on goods from Massachusetts than from Britain.[48]

It certainly appears as if the American people opposed British mercantilism out of self interest, not out of principle. When tariffs could be used to serve their own interests, the people demanded the same protectionist policies they previously rebelled against. With democratically elected politicians pandering to the voters, merchants and laborers alike lobbied their state governments to favor their particular good or service. Whereas before the War for Independence, Americans complained about British tariffs; after the war, the British complained about America's mercantilist policies.[49]

Because shippers easily avoided the tariffs, these taxes brought in little revenue. James Madison explained, "It will dissipate every prospect of drawing a steady revenue from our imposts either directly into the federal treasury, or indirectly thro' the treasuries of the Commercial States, and of consequence the former must depend for supplies solely on annual requisitions, and the latter on direct taxes drawn from the property of the Country." Madison added that these tariffs were an "anarchy of our commerces" and that "most of our political evils may be traced up to our commercial ones."[50]

In addition to tariffs, states had other methods of favoring its citizens over those of other states. State governments failed to enforce contracts when it benefited their residents and printed money to excess, thereby, devaluing their own currency.[51] As Alexander Hamilton wrote, "It is known, that the relaxed conduct of the state Governments in regard to property & credit was one of the most serious diseases under which the body politic laboured prior to the adoption of our present constitution and was a material cause of that state of public opinion which led to its adoption."[52]

As a result of these trade wars, there was much fear of civil war between the states, especially between New York and its neighboring states of New Jersey and Connecticut. New Jersey and Connecticut both relied on New York Harbor for much of its trade and New York taxed those states heavily.

John Jay even worried that these trade wars might invite foreign involvement in domestic disputes: "It would be more natural for these confederacies to apprehend danger from one another than from distant nations, and therefore that each of them should be more desirous to guard against the others by the aid of foreign alliances, than to guard against foreign dangers by alliances between themselves."[53]

The states threatened war over these trade disputes, but none were ever fought. In contrast, there were real wars fought over conflicting territorial claims. Six colonies had charters that granted them all land to the west within certain latitudes. Three states claimed land that was not even contiguous to the rest of the state.[54] Various states had overlapping territorial claims and, in some instances, three states claimed the same land.[55] This brought the states into conflict with one another or with settlers in the western territories who recognized one state's claim but not that of another.

Pennsylvania and Connecticut both claimed possession of the Wyoming Valley in current-day Pennsylvania. Settlers from those two states fought a series of battles over the land. New York and Massachusetts argued about the land between the Hudson River and Connecticut River. New York was also in a dispute with New Hampshire over Vermont. Another dispute occurred regarding 29 million acres that North Carolina gave to Congress in 1784 but rescinded a few months later. In the meantime, the people living there established the State of Franklin, which operated as an independent republic for four years.

While the states were reluctant to give up their claims, they were even more reluctant to go to war with each other. The states compromised and ceded their territorial claims as part of the Northwest Ordinance. This solved some of the land disputes, but not all of them. The Pennamite War between Connecticut and Pennsylvania over the Wyoming Valley was not fully resolved until 1799. The State of Franklin was not reacquired by North Carolina until 1788, but was then given to the federal government in 1790, and became part of the state of Tennessee in 1796.

The Founding Fathers also complained about the multiplicity and mutability of state laws. James Madison spoke against this "evil" before, during, and after the Constitutional Convention. In April 1787, just prior to the Convention, Madison wrote, "Among the evils then of our situation may well be ranked the multiplicity of laws from which no State is exempt… The short period of independency has filled as many pages as the century which preceded it. Every year, almost every session, adds a new volume." Madison then turned to the "mutability of the laws of the States" and wrote, "This evil is intimately connected with the former yet deserves a distinct notice as it emphatically denotes a vicious legislation. We daily see laws repealed or superseded, before any trial can have been made of their merits: and even before a knowledge of them can have reached the remoter districts within which they were to operate. In the regulations of trade this instability becomes a snare not only to our citizens but to foreigners also."[56]

At the conclusion of the Constitutional Convention, Madison expressed the same sentiment in a letter to Thomas Jefferson. Madison wrote, "The mutability of the laws of the States is found to be a serious evil. The injustice of them has been so frequent and so flagrant as to alarm the most stedfast friends of Republicanism."[57]

In February 1788, Madison wrote about this in Federalist No. 62: "It will be of little avail to the people, that the laws are made by men of their own choice, if the laws be so voluminous that they cannot be read, or so incoherent that they cannot be understood; if they be repealed or revised before they are promulgated, or undergo such incessant changes that no man, who knows what the law is to-day, can guess what it will be to-morrow."

To fight the tyranny of the state governments, Madison proposed giving the federal government the power to veto state laws. In a letter to George Washington just prior to the Constitutional Convention, Madison wrote that giving Congress the power to veto state legislation "appears to me to be absolutely necessary" or else "the States will continue to invade the National jurisdiction, to violate treaties and the law of nations & to harass each other with rival and spiteful measures dictated by mistaken views of interest."[58] To Jefferson, he wrote, "A constitutional negative on the laws of the States seems equally necessary to secure individuals against encroachments on their rights."[59] When the Convention failed to include this veto power in the Constitution, Madison argued that without this power, "the plan, should it be adopted, will neither effectually answer its national object, nor prevent the local mischiefs which everywhere excite disgusts against the State Governments."[60] Although the delegates to the Constitutional Convention rejected Madison's idea of a federal veto over state laws because they feared a powerful federal government, they did place significant checks on the states to prevent the infringement of individual rights by the states and to protect the states from each other.

PEACE WITHOUT SECURITY

The Treaty of Paris was the greatest accomplishment of the Confederation government. Gordon Wood even calls it "the greatest achievement in the history of American diplomacy."[61] Like in the War for Independence, America successfully played the European nations against one another in the peace negotiations to win the best terms. All the European nations wanted America as an ally and to do business with the growing country. Thomas Paine had predicted this in *Common Sense*: "Our plan is commerce, and that, well attended to, will secure us the peace and friendship of all Europe; because it is the interest of all Europe to have America a free port. Her trade will always be a protection."[62]

With the war over, the power of Congress decreased. War always increases the power of government, so Congress's power naturally declined after the war ended. As Thomas Jefferson wrote shortly after the signing of the Treaty of Paris: "The constant session of Congress cannot be necessary in time of peace, and their separation will destroy the strange idea of their being a permanent body, which has unaccountably taken possession of the heads of their constituents, and occasions jealousies injurious to the public good."[63] As a result of Congress's diminished power and stature, many delegates lost interest and Congress had difficulty gathering a quorum.

Congress, already short on funds and seen by many to be unnecessary, had little choice but to reduce expenditures. The Confederation government eliminated the navy, reduced the army to almost nothing, and failed to pay army pensions. The government defaulted on its debts to France when it stopped making interest payments in 1785 and failed to repay principal due in 1787.[64] The Confederation government was bankrupt according to all measures. America was left with no defensive capabilities except for an armed citizenry, the ocean separating America from Europe, and its commercial ties. It had no means of raising an army or navy, even though the European nations were already threatening America's sovereignty.

Even with the war over, the Treaty of Paris signed, and Britain removed from the thirteen states, America was vulnerable. Britain still had troops in Canada and never left the Northwest Territory as agreed to in the Treaty of Paris because the United States failed to restore all Loyalist property as it had promised. Britain plotted with the Indians against America and promoted separatist movements along America's border with Canada.

Spain also took advantage of America's weaknesses. Spain encouraged separatist movements in the Southwest. Spain refused to recognize American sovereignty over the land south of the Ohio River and west of the Appalachians because the Treaty of Paris did not delineate the northern boundary for Spanish Florida. In 1784, Spain closed the Mississippi River to the United States, even though Article 8 of the Treaty of Paris explicitly states, "The navigation of the river Mississippi, from its source to the ocean, shall forever remain free and open to the subjects of Great Britain and the citizens of the United States."[65]

Lacking an army and a powerful central government, the Confederation could not argue its claims nor defend them with force. The states could negotiate but they had little to offer Britain and even less to bargain with Spain. John Jay tried to negotiate with Spain on behalf of the states, but an agreement was never reached, in part because Jay realized he could never get the required nine of thirteen states to agree to a treaty.

Alexander Hamilton explained America's impotence on the world stage:

> Are we in a condition to resent or to repel the aggression? We have neither troops, nor treasury, nor government. Are we even in a condition to remonstrate with dignity? The just imputations on our own faith, in respect to the same treaty, ought first to be removed. Are we entitled by nature and compact to a free participation in the navigation of the Mississippi? Spain excludes us from it. Is public credit an indispensable resource in time of public danger? We seem to have abandoned its cause as desperate and irretrievable. Is commerce of importance to national wealth? Ours is at the lowest point of declension. Is respectability in the eyes of foreign powers a safeguard against foreign encroachments? The imbecility of our government even forbids them to treat with us. Our ambassadors abroad are the mere pageants of mimic sovereignty.[66]

America was vulnerable on all fronts and the European powers were not afraid to exploit those weaknesses.

Even though America defeated Britain and won independence, the peace was fragile. America's borders were uncertain and enemies all around were ready to attack or subvert American sovereignty. At the same time, America had disbanded its army, the Confederation was bankrupt, and the bickering states could never agree long enough to negotiate successfully with Britain or Spain. Though the war was won, America's future was more insecure than it had been before the colonists rebelled against Britain.

REVOLUTION AT RISK

For all the hard work, money, and lives spent defeating the British, the American Revolution could easily have been a complete failure. Independence did not result in immediate success as many had hoped and expected. Independence only enabled success, but did not guarantee it. This great opportunity was being squandered by the weak Articles of Confederation, disagreements among the states, and the inability to rein in the angry mobs.

Without a stable government, independence would have been quite meaningless. Looking back at the revolution he helped launch, Thomas Paine wrote in 1791, "The Independence of America, considered merely as a separation from England, would have been a matter of but little importance, had it not been accompanied by a Revolution in the principles and practice of Governments."[67] Actually, independence without a stable government was in many ways worse than living under British rule because of the chaos and insecurity under the Confederation and state governments. The states infringed upon individual rights just as the British had and put up protective tariffs just as Britain had. Angry mobs ran wild with their riots, conspiracies, mutinies, and rebellions, just as they had before America declared independence.

Despite the increase in America's population and the country's westward expansion, America was not much better off under the Confederation than it had been under Britain. Economic growth was weak, the monetary system was in shambles, the government was deep in debt, credit was nonexistent, and the nation had no defensive capabilities. By 1787, six years after defeating Britain, eleven years after declaring independence, and more than twenty years after first protesting against British oppression, this grand experiment was largely unsuccessful and could fall apart at any moment.

The angry mobs produced their revolution and succeeded to a limited extent. It would be up to the Founding Fathers, who had already done so much to ensure victory over the British and to maintain law and order, to create a working political system and secure peace and tranquility for generations to come.

CHAPTER FIVE

CREATING THE CONSTITUTION

T o overthrow a government is common. Thousands of societies have done so. Domestic and foreign rulers have been deposed. Monarchies and democratic governments have both been ousted from power. In the end, all governments eventually fall and are replaced by new ones.

When America defeated Britain in the War for Independence and the states established new governments in the late 1770s, there was nothing revolutionary about it. Some of the ideas on which they based their desire for sovereignty were revolutionary, but the act of rebellion was not.

The more significant revolution came long after America declared and won independence. This revolution occurred only after a period of significant struggles for the new nation. The Constitution was the real revolution, perhaps the most revolutionary event in the history of the world. To establish a lasting constitution and government "from reflection and choice"[1] is unique in the history of mankind.

The Constitution that today is recognized around the world as a brilliant creation was the cause of much debate back in its day. Based on the study of history and political philosophy, the Founding Fathers invented a new and untested political system. Many Americans in 1787 were afraid of this unknown quantity. However, after the chaos under the Articles of Confederation, the American people reluctantly agreed to this grand experiment.

CALLING FOR A CONVENTION

Just six years after becoming the law of the land, many Americans realized the Articles of Confederation were broken. The states were unable to reach consensus, unwilling to give money to the Congress of the Confederation, and unable to pay the soldiers, except with worthless paper money.[2] Meanwhile, Congress was powerless to fix these problems. Alexander Hamilton described the years under the Articles of Confederation as "an unequivocal experience of the inefficacy of the subsisting federal government."[3]

The inadequacies of the political system to deal with America's problems prompted calls to amend the Articles of Confederation. The Annapolis Convention of September 1786 was a failure with only five states attending. A second convention was called for Philadelphia in May 1787. All thirteen states attended this second convention because Shays' Rebellion in late 1786 and early 1787 convinced them of the inadequacies of the Articles of Confederation. The delegates to this Philadelphia Convention still had to decide whether to amend the Articles of Confederation or write a brand new constitution, but all agreed that the government needed fixing.

The primary purpose of the Constitutional Convention was to weaken the state governments and give the national government the power it needed to fulfill its responsibilities. Under the Articles of Confederation, the federal government had "no authority" and its laws were "mere recommendations which the States observe or disregard at their option."[4] Additionally, the states were too strong and too democratic, leading to "tyranny of the majority" and "democratic despotism."[5]

The goal of the convention was not to make a stronger government in general, but to shift power from the states to the national government. The power of government would remain the same, but the state governments and national government would become more equal and would provide better checks on one another. As Gordon Wood explains in *The American Revolution: A History*, "The reconstruction of the central government was being sought as a means of correcting not only the weaknesses of the Articles but also the democratic despotism and internal political abuses of the states." The goal was not only to save Congress from the states, but also to "save the states from themselves." The Founding Fathers "saw themselves rather as saving the Revolution from its excesses."[6]

The Constitutional Convention would also try to unify the country's economy and end the trade disputes between the states. In fact, the Annapolis Convention of 1786 was called "to consider how far a uniform system in their commercial regulations and other important matters might be necessary to the common interest and permanent harmony of the several states."[7] The Constitutional Convention in Philadelphia also sought to solve this problem. The Founders wished to create an economic system in which the government's only roles were to encourage free trade and protect property rights. In other words, they wanted to end the protectionist policies of the states.

The Constitutional Convention took years of planning. Alexander Hamilton called for a convention as far back as 1780 and started working with James Madison in 1782 to strengthen the national government.[8] Year after year, powerful state politicians, such as Patrick Henry of Virginia and George Clinton of New York, resisted calls for a stronger central government. In the end, though, the economic depression, currency devaluation, defensive vulnerability, trade wars, and rebellions by angry mobs forced a convention. During the War for Independence, the people focused on defeating Britain and ignored the deficiencies of the Articles of Confederation and the state governments. With the war over, America could no longer overlook these problems. America had, as Hamilton described it, "reached almost the last stage of national humiliation. There is scarcely anything that can wound the pride or degrade the character of an independent nation which we do not experience."[9]

In such a weak condition, America was finally ready for the change that the Founding Fathers had been seeking for years. Even still, the grand experiment that the Founders were about to embark upon would meet much resistance from a large portion of the population. The anarchic and democratic nature of the angry mobs had not yet been subdued and some of the political leaders of the states were not willing to sacrifice their power and influence.

AN ASSEMBLY OF DEMIGODS

Twelve years after the American Revolution began at Lexington and Concord, the country was descending into chaos. The Articles of

Confederation failed to govern, the government was deep in debt, and thousands of soldiers had not been paid for their service during the war. Fifty-five men gathered in Philadelphia in the summer of 1787 to save the young nation.

Americans were on edge as the delegates met behind closed doors to decide the fate of millions of people. America had already achieved so much in just a few years: the Declaration of Independence, fighting so bravely in the War for Independence, and the victory over Britain. But all these great achievements would be for nothing if they could not create a stable government.

In a letter to John Adams, Thomas Jefferson called the delegates of the Constitutional Convention "an assembly of demigods."[10] Jefferson wrote this even before the Constitution was completed and, because the convention met behind closed doors, which Jefferson complained about, he had no idea what was being discussed or what the Constitution would look like when completed. Nevertheless, Jefferson wrote that he had "no doubt that all their other measures will be good and wise."[11]

These great men, each of whom was capable of holding high office, put aside their personal aspirations and did what they thought best for their respective states and the nation. James Madison writes, "There was never an assembly of men, charged with a great & arduous trust, who were more pure in their motives, or more exclusively or anxiously [devoted to the object committed to them, than were the members of the Federal Convention of 1787, to the object of devising and proposing a constitutional system which would best supply the defects of that which it was to replace, and best secure the permanent liberty and happiness of their country.]"[12]

Alexis de Tocqueville concurs, "The assembly which was responsible for the drafting of the second constitution, though small in number, contained the finest minds and the noblest characters that had ever emerged in the New World." He adds, "The people chose, not perhaps men they loved most but those that they held in the highest esteem... The legislators of the Union had almost all been remarkable for their intelligence and even more so for their patriotism."[13]

Most of the delegates were wealthy, well educated, and politically experienced. More than half had college educations at a time when fewer than one-tenth of one percent attended college. Forty-five were wealthy. Twelve earned their fortunes while thirty-one were born rich and two married into wealth. The group included businessmen, plantation owners, physicians, and professors. Eight signed the Declaration of Independence, thirty-nine served in the Continental Congress, eight helped write state constitutions, seven had been governors, thirty-four were lawyers, and a third had served in the Continental Army. To add to the prestige of the group, the retired George Washington reluctantly agreed to attend the Convention and act as its President, for fear that some would think he opposed it if he were absent.[14]

Initially, there were two camps in the Convention. Some wanted to strengthen the Congress but maintain the Confederation whereas others wanted to abandon the Confederation and form a national republic. William Paterson introduced the New Jersey Plan to strengthen Congress but maintain the Confederation. James Madison proposed the Virginia Plan to create a new national republic. The supporters of the Virginia Plan even proposed giving the new national government the power "to legislate in all cases to which the separate states are incompetent" and "to negative all laws passed by the several States contravening, in the opinion of the national Legislature, the articles of union, or any treaties subsisting under the authority of the Union."[15] In the end, neither plan was followed, but a national republic was created "to form a more perfect Union, establish Justice, insure domestic Tranquility, provide for the common defence, promote the general Welfare, and secure the Blessings of Liberty to ourselves and our Posterity."[16]

Nobody at the Constitutional Convention got everything he wanted, but through debate and compromise the new Constitution satisfied nearly all the delegates. At the end of the contentious four-month convention, thirty-nine delegates signed the Constitution. Though there were a few dissenters—many of whom wanted a bill of rights, a deficiency that was easily remedied—the vast majority of the delegates supported the final product and it was approved with the "Unanimous Consent of the States present."[17] Nevertheless, the fight over the Constitution's ratification would be even more difficult than the creation of the document itself.

CONSTITUTIONAL GOALS

In drafting a new constitution, the primary goal was to secure the rights of man, as is the goal of all republican governments. The Declaration of Independence explains, "We hold these truths to be self-evident, that all men are created equal, that they are endowed by their Creator with certain unalienable Rights, that among these are Life, Liberty and the pursuit of Happiness. – That to secure these rights, Governments are instituted among Men."

All the delegates agreed that this was the purpose of government. The only question was how best to secure those rights. At the Constitutional Convention, Roger Sherman remarked, "The question is, not what rights naturally belong to men; but how they may be most equally & effectually guarded in Society."[18]

To start, the Founding Fathers recognized that the people were the source of all power and no system of government could be maintained without their support. As the Declaration of Independence states, "Governments are instituted among Men, deriving their just powers from the consent of the governed." Starting with the words "We the People of the United States," the Constitution recognizes that power comes from the people, not from the Constitutional Convention, Congress, or the states. Madison confirmed these sentiments when he wrote in three different Federalist Papers:

The people are the only legitimate fountain of power.[19]

The ultimate authority, wherever the derivative may be found, resides in the people alone.[20]

We may define a republic to be, or at least may bestow that name on, a government which derives all its powers directly or indirectly from the great body of the people.[21]

The state constitutions express the same principle. The Constitution of Massachusetts, written by John Adams in 1779, states, "All power residing originally in the people, and being derived from them, the several magistrates and officers of government…are their substitutes and agents, and are at all times accountable to them." More recent constitutions proclaim this as well. For example, the Arizona Constitution states, "All political power is inherent in the people, and governments derive their just powers from the consent of the governed, and are established to protect and maintain individual rights."

Not only does power derive from the people, in the end, it stays with the people. Just as only the people can create governments, only the people can support or restrain them. Madison explains, "A dependence on the people is, no doubt, the primary control on the government."[22] He adds that a constitution would only be a "parchment barrier" if the people fail to support it.[23] Madison also writes, "A mere demarcation on parchment of the constitutional limits of the several departments, is not a sufficient guard against those encroachments which lead to a tyrannical concentration of all the powers of government in the same hands."[24] Jefferson agrees, "Our peculiar security is in the possession of a written Constitution. Let us not make it a blank paper by construction."[25]

Even though the Founding Fathers recognized that power is derived from the consent of the governed, they knew of the evils of unchecked power in the hands of the majority. The Founders recognized that pure democracy was just another form of despotism. In fact, "democratic despotism" is even worse than the despotism of an individual or foreign power because democratic despotism gains legitimacy by proclaiming itself to be the will of the people.[26]

The previous twenty years gave the Founding Fathers firsthand experience in "democratic despotism" as angry mobs overthrew British colonial rule, threatened Congress and the state governments, and used the state governments for their own benefit at the expense of other states and minority factions. With their knowledge of political history[27] and firsthand experience with the angry mobs, the Founding Fathers repeatedly expressed a distrust of the public's ability to govern themselves.

Though the American people loved and admired George Washington, he did not trust the people to create or manage government. In May 1786, Washington wrote to the Marquis de Lafayette, "It is one of the evils of democratical governments, that the people, not always seeing and frequently misled, must often feel before they can act."[28] In September 1786, Washington argued that democracy could not work because the people cannot "possess that knowledge which is necessary for them to decide" and would not be "present at all the information and arguments, which would come forward." Instead, it is "much wiser and more politic, to choose able and honest representatives, and leave them in all national questions to determine from the evidence of reason, and the facts which shall be adduced."[29]

James Madison, the architect of the Constitution, also warned against democratic government. At the Constitutional Convention, Madison argued, "Where a majority are united by a common sentiment, and have an opportunity, the rights of the minor party become insecure."[30] He repeated this in Federalist No. 51, stating, "If a majority be united by a common interest, the rights of the minority will be insecure." Madison also believed that "democracies have ever been spectacles of turbulence and contention; have ever been found incompatible with personal security or the rights of property; and have in general been as short in their lives as they have been violent in their deaths."[31]

Madison not only feared the tyranny of the majority, but also overactive and incompetent government. He had seen the "multiplicity" and "mutability" of state laws[32] and argued that this alone, even without abusive intent, created problems. In Federalist No. 62, Madison wrote:

> Another effect of public instability is the unreasonable advantage it gives to the sagacious, the enterprising, and the moneyed few over the industrious and uninformed mass of the people. Every new regulation concerning commerce or revenue, or in any way affecting the value of the different species of property, presents a new harvest to those who watch the change, and can trace its consequences; a harvest, reared not by themselves, but by the toils and cares of the great body of their fellow-citizens. This is a state of things in which it may be said with some truth that laws are made for the few, not for the many.

In another point of view, great injury results from an un-
stable government. The want of confidence in the public
councils damps every useful undertaking, the success and
profit of which may depend on a continuance of existing ar-
rangements. What prudent merchant will hazard his fortunes in any new branch of commerce when he knows not
but that his plans may be rendered unlawful before they can
be executed? What farmer or manufacturer will lay himself
out for the encouragement given to any particular cultiva-
tion or establishment, when he can have no assurance that
his preparatory labors and advances will not render him a
victim to an inconstant government? In a word, no great
improvement or laudable enterprise can go forward which
requires the auspices of a steady system of national policy.

Thomas Jefferson also argued that limits had to be placed on democratic principles to protect the minority from the majority. In his first
inaugural address of March 1801, Jefferson stated, "All, too, will bear in
mind this sacred principle, that though the will of the majority is in all
cases to prevail, that will, to be rightful, must be reasonable; that the
minority possess their equal rights, which equal laws must protect, and
to violate would be oppression."[33]

Other Founding Fathers used even stronger language in their attacks
on the democratic ideal. Alexander Hamilton argued at the Constitutional Convention, "If we incline too much to democracy, we shall soon
shoot into a monarchy."[34] John Jay argued in 1809, "Pure democracy, like
pure rum, easily produces intoxication, and with it a thousand mad
pranks and fooleries."[35] At the Massachusetts Ratifying Convention in
1788, Fisher Ames argued, "A democracy is a volcano, which conceals the
fiery materials of its own destruction. These will produce an eruption,
and carry desolation in their way."[36]

Though the Founders saw the evils of mob rule, they also wished to
harness its energy. They wanted to turn the passions of the people into a
supporter and protector of the new government instead of an enemy
against it. Therefore, the Founding Fathers wanted to limit but not

eliminate the democratic nature of their new republican government. They wanted to create a moderate government, one that balanced rule of law with the democratic nature of the American people.

At the Constitutional Convention, Alexander Hamilton said, "We are now forming a republican government. Real liberty is neither found in despotism, nor in the extremes of democracy, but in moderate governments."[37] Hamilton also believed that it was the job of the Founding Fathers "to vindicate the honor of the human race, and to teach that assuming brother, moderation."[38] Hamilton hoped the new Constitution would create "the perfect balance between liberty and power."[39]

Alexis de Tocqueville also wrote about the Founding Fathers' efforts to find this balance: "They profoundly felt a sincere and warm affection for this very liberty; they dared to voice their desire to restrain it because they certainly did not wish to destroy it."[40]

To secure the rights of man, restrain the democratic impulses of society, and form a "moderate" government, the Founding Fathers established a government of laws. True liberty can only be found where the laws are fixed because, as John Adams explains, "No man will contend that a nation can be free that is not governed by fixed laws. All other government than that of permanent known laws, is the government of mere will and pleasure, whether it be exercised by one, a few, or many."[41]

To prevent ambitious politicians or groups from gaining control over the whole of government, the Founding Fathers recognized the need for a system of checks and balances. As Madison argued, "The great security against a gradual concentration of the several powers in the same department, consists in giving to those who administer each department the necessary constitutional means and personal motives to resist encroachments of the others. The provision for defense must in this, as in all other cases, be made commensurate to the danger of attack. Ambition must be made to counteract ambition."[42]

In the end, even with systems of checks and balances, the Founding Fathers recognized that only the people could prevent tyranny by the national or state governments. Alexander Hamilton wrote that if the Constitution is violated, "A remedy must be obtained from the people who can, by the election of more faithful representatives, annul the acts of the usurpers."[43] If that fails, Madison prescribes other means: "If the representatives of the people betray their constituents, there is then no recourse left but in the exertion of that original right of self-defense which is paramount to all positive forms of government... The citizens must rush tumultuously to arms, without concert, without system, without resource; except in their courage and despair."[44]

Although Hamilton, Madison, and the Founding Fathers designed a Constitution that they hoped would make such actions unnecessary, they recognized that, in the end, the people are the "ultimate guardians of their own liberty."[45]

CHECKS AND BALANCES

The Founding Fathers distrusted all political power. As James Madison wrote, "All power in human hands is liable to be abused."[46] To prevent any individual, faction, state, or branch of government from gaining too much power, the Founding Fathers created an elaborate system of checks and balances. Madison explained, "The powers of government should be so divided and balanced among several bodies of magistracy, as that no one could transcend their legal limits, without being effectually checked and restrained by the others."[47]

Charles de Secondat Montesquieu, the most cited political thinker at the time of the American Revolution,[48] was a major proponent of checks and balances and proposed a tripartite system of government with political power divided among executive, legislative, and judicial branches. This idea of checks and balances existed for thousands of years, but in different forms. The ancient Greek historian Polybius, also widely read by the Founding Fathers,[49] described the balance of power between the people, Senate, and magistrates in ancient Rome nearly two thousand years earlier. Polybius wrote, "None of the three is absolute, but the purpose of the one can be counterworked and thwarted by the others, none of them will excessively outgrow the others or treat them with contempt. All in fact remains in statu quo, on the one hand, because any aggressive impulse is sure to be checked and from the outset each estate stands in dread of being interfered with by the others."[50] Likewise,

Montesquieu wrote, "The government of Rome was admirable. From its birth, abuses of power could always be corrected by its constitution, whether by means of the spirit of the people, the strength of the senate, or the authority of certain magistrates."[51]

History and political philosophy taught the Founding Fathers that checks and balances must be the centerpiece of their new system. George Washington explained in his Farewell Address of 1796: "The necessity of reciprocal checks in the exercise of political power, by dividing and distributing it into different depositaries, and constituting each the guardian of the public weal against invasions by the others, has been evinced by experiments ancient and modern; some of them in our country and under our own eyes."[52]

The Founding Fathers took this idea to new extremes, creating a system with multiple levels of checks and balances. After experiencing the tyranny of a strong central government under British rule and the tyranny of the states under the Articles of Confederation, the Founders wanted to avoid both by creating checks and balances between the states and federal government. To do so, they had to invent a new system of dual sovereignty. Madison explained the uniqueness of this system, "Every previous national authority either had been centralized or else had been a confederation of sovereign states. The new American system was neither one nor the other; it was a mixture of both."[53]

The goal of this federalist system was to balance the powers of the states against that of the federal government and to give each checks on the other. Hamilton explained, "Power being almost always the rival of power, the general government will at all times stand ready to check the usurpations of the state governments, and these will have the same disposition towards the general government. The people, by throwing themselves into either scale, will infallibly make it preponderate. If their rights are invaded by either, they can make use of the other as the instrument of redress."[54] Madison added, "Hence a double security arises to the rights of the people. The different governments will control each other, at the same time that each will be controlled by itself."[55] Hamilton borrowed Madison's arguments and even some of his words for the New York Ratifying Convention, at which he said that "this balance between the National and State governments" was "of the utmost importance. It forms a double security to the people. If one encroaches on their rights they will find a powerful protection in the other. Indeed, they will both be prevented from overpassing their constitutional limits by a certain rivalship, which will ever subsist between them."[56]

Even with the states and federal government checking each other, the Founding Fathers purposely skewed the balance of power in favor of the states. Although the experiences of state tyranny under the Articles of Confederation were fresh in their minds, even more so Americans did not want a powerful central government like they had with Britain. The Founding Fathers also recognized that state tyranny is more manageable than federal tyranny because, in most cases, state tyranny affects only the citizens of that state. People could easily move between the states, fleeing the more tyrannical states to go to the more free ones. In contrast, federal tyranny would be more difficult to escape. Most of all, though, the Founders had to keep most of the power with the states because the states would have opposed ratification if the Constitution gave too much power to the federal government.

The Founding Fathers argued throughout the ratification debate that the power of the states would exceed that of the federal government under the Constitution. James Wilson pointed out that the federal government could not even exist without the states: "The President is to be chosen by electors, nominated in such manner as the legislature of each State may direct; so that if there is no legislature there can be no electors, and consequently the office of President cannot be supplied. The Senate is to be composed of two Senators from each State, chosen by the Legislature; and, therefore, if there is no Legislature, there can be no Senate. The House of Representatives is to be composed of members chosen every second year by the people of the several States, and the electors in each State shall have the qualifications requisite for electors of the most numerous branch of the State Legislature; unless, therefore, there is a State Legislature, that qualification cannot be ascertained, and the popular branch of the federal constitution must be extinct."[57]

Madison and Hamilton explained how the states would be more powerful than the federal government under the Constitution. Madison wrote, "The powers delegated by the proposed Constitution to the federal government, are few and defined. Those which are to remain in the State governments are numerous and indefinite." He then argued, "The State governments will have the advantage of the Federal government, whether we compare them in respect to the immediate dependence of the one on the other; to the weight of personal influence which each side will possess; to the powers respectively vested in them; to the predilection and probable support of the people; to the disposition and faculty of resisting and frustrating the measures of each other."[58]

Hamilton made the same argument, "It will always be far more easy for the State governments to encroach upon the national authorities than for the national government to encroach upon the State authorities."[59] Hamilton added, "We may safely rely on the disposition of the State legislatures to erect barriers against the encroachments of the national authority."[60] Madison even worried that "the plan, should it be adopted, will neither effectually answer its national object, nor prevent the local mischiefs which everywhere excite disgusts against the State Governments."[61]

Alexis de Tocqueville confirms that the states were indeed more powerful than the federal government nearly half a century later. Tocqueville writes in *Democracy in America*, "State government remains the general rule, the federal government is the exception."[62] Tocqueville adds, "In America real power resides in provincial government rather more than in federal government."[63] And confirming Hamilton's assertion that the people will decide whether the states or federal government will dominate, Tocqueville writes, "The passions of the masses and the provincial bias of every state still tend strangely to reduce the scope of federal power as it is laid down and to create pockets of resistance to its wishes."[64]

The statistics also appear to confirm the relative weakness of the federal government. State and local government spending exceeded federal spending in most years until the 1940s, except in war time.[65] Based on this one metric, the state and local governments exerted more power than the federal government for about 150 years, except in the power to declare and make war.

The predominant feature of the Constitution is the federal government's division into three branches, just as Montesquieu recommended.

John Jay succinctly summarized this separation of powers: "Let Congress legislate, let others execute, let others judge."[66] Madison explained the necessity for three separate branches: "The accumulation of all powers, legislative, executive, and judiciary, in the same hands, whether of one, a few, or many, and whether hereditary, selfappointed, or elective, may justly be pronounced the very definition of tyranny."[67]

The Founding Fathers believed the legislative branch to be the most dangerous of all and added extra checks and balances on it. As Madison explained, "The legislative department is everywhere extending the sphere of its activity, and drawing all power into its impetuous vortex... Its constitutional powers being at once more extensive, and less suscepti-ble of precise limits, it can, with the greater facility, mask, under compli-cated and indirect measures, the encroachments which it makes on the co-ordinate departments... The legislative department alone has access to the pockets of the people."[68]

Therefore, the Founding Fathers split the legislative branch into two houses to diffuse its power. Britain and the states already had two legislative houses and the Founders agreed that those bicameral systems were superior to unicameral legislatures. However, there was much disagreement at the Constitutional Convention regarding how the two houses would represent the people. One group argued that both houses should have an equal number of representatives for each state whereas another group argued for representation proportional to population. Roger Sherman and Oliver Ellsworth, both of Connecticut, proposed a compromise wherein House seats would be allocated in proportion to the population of each state but each state would control an equal number of Senate seats. Additionally, the people would directly elect representatives to the House, whereas state legislatures would choose its two senators. Furthermore, representatives would serve two-year terms while senators serve for six years. As a result, the House would be close to the people and represent them, whereas the Senate would represent the states. The smaller, more exclusive Senate would be a check on the more democratic House of Representatives.

This compromise was quite ingenious. As Madison explained, "In republican government, the legislative authority necessarily predominates. The remedy for this inconveniency is to divide the legislature into different branches; and to render them, by different modes of election and different principles of action, as little connected with each other as the nature of their common functions and their common dependence on the society will admit."[69]

With two different methods of selecting the members of the two houses of Congress, it would be more difficult for any faction to gain control of both. Additionally, the President would be selected by a third method—the electoral college—and serve for four years. And the judges would be chosen by a fourth method—Presidential appointment with the consent of the Senate—and serve for life. With the different methods of selection and different terms of service, it would be nearly impossible for a single faction to control all three branches of government.

As another check on the legislative branch, the Constitution gave the President the power to veto legislation passed by Congress. With this, the President can stop Congress's most egregious bills from becoming law. However, a two-thirds majority of both houses of Congress can vote to overturn the Presidential veto, thus preventing the President from blocking all legislation, which would have taken away all of Congress's power.

Even with this elaborate system of checks and balances, the Founding Fathers realized that, as Tocqueville would write, "Absolute perfection is almost never a feature of a system of laws."[70] They knew the Constitution was not perfect and would need changing as flaws were discovered. The Founding Fathers, therefore, provided a way to amend the Constitution that allows for vital updates but prevents constant alteration. Constitutional amendments require a two-thirds vote in each house of Congress and ratification by three-quarters of the states.[71] After the states ratified the Bill of Rights in 1791, the Constitution has been amended just seventeen times, making it a remarkably stable document.

The Constitution did include one serious flaw. According to the Constitution, in the Presidential election, each elector in the electoral college casts two votes with the winner becoming President and the runner-up Vice President. In the case of a tie, the election goes to the House of Representatives where each state gets one vote. In 1800, Thomas Jefferson and his running mate Aaron Burr each won seventy-three electoral votes. It took thirty-six rounds of voting in the House before Jefferson won a majority of the states. This problem was fixed by the Twelfth Amendment, which was proposed in December 1803 and ratified just six months later, by separating the votes for President and Vice President. Despite its flaws, the Constitution was strong enough to survive challenges, yet flexible enough to correct its deficiencies.

SLAVERY AND THE CONSTITUTION

One of the most frequent criticisms of the Constitution was its failure to abolish slavery. The Marquis de Lafayette reportedly said, "I would never have drawn my sword in the cause of America if I could have conceived thereby that I was founding a land of slavery."[72] With the passing decades and centuries, the criticism of the Founding Fathers regarding slavery has only increased.

Even though the Founding Fathers failed to abolish slavery, most of them recognized the evils of that institution and pointed out that slavery would divide the nation if it were allowed to remain.[73] At the Constitutional Convention, James Madison argued that slavery was the primary division between the states[74] and said that "the mere distinction of colour made in the most enlightened period of time" was "a ground of the most oppressive dominion ever exercised by man over man."[75]

While Southerners like Madison recognized the evils of slavery and would have liked, in theory, to abolish the institution, most of them did nothing to aid the abolitionist cause. Most of the Southern Founding Fathers, including Washington, Jefferson, and Madison, struggled with their ownership of slaves even as they announced to the world that "all men are created equal."

In contrast, many of the Northern delegates actively fought against slavery. The Northern states were the first in history to eliminate slavery through legislation, starting with Vermont in 1777.[76] Many of the Founding Fathers supported and led the abolitionist movement in the North, including Benjamin Franklin, who headed the Pennsylvania Abolition Society, and John Jay, Aaron Burr, and Alexander Hamilton, who all belonged to the New York Manumission Society. These Founders worked tirelessly to free the slaves, but abolishing slavery was no easy task.

Even in the North, not everybody supported abolition and some who did were still concerned about the effects it would have on their society. Northerners worried about an influx of blacks from the South taking their jobs, requiring economic support, and stealing to support themselves. They also worried that an influx of free blacks would lead to whites and blacks mingling and intermarrying. Consequently, even the Northern states restricted the immigration of blacks and disenfranchised many free blacks.[77] In a nation where the South did not want to free their slaves and the North did not want to see an influx of black immigrants, abolishing slavery would have gone against the wishes of the majority of Americans.

As was evident throughout the American Revolution, the Founding Fathers had to stay attuned to the demands of the common people. In fact, many times the angry mobs led the way and the Founding Fathers followed. Though the Founding Fathers had the opportunity to put their intellect and experience to work at the Constitutional Convention, they could not create a new system the people would disagree with because the Constitution needed approval from the people at the state ratifying conventions. Perhaps, if the Founding Fathers could have created their ideal Constitution, they would have abolished slavery. Instead, they were forced to create a constitution for the society that existed.

Eleven years earlier, the Founding Fathers experienced similar opposition to the mere mention of the evils of slavery. In his rough draft of the Declaration of Independence, Thomas Jefferson blamed King George III for slavery in America:

> He has waged cruel war against human nature itself, violating its most sacred rights of life and liberty in the persons of a distant people who never offended him, captivating and carrying them into slavery in another hemisphere, or to incur miserable death in their transportation thither. This piratical warfare, the opprobrium of infidel powers, is the warfare of the Christian king of Great Britain. Determined to keep open a market where men should be bought

and sold, he has prostituted his negative for suppressing every legislative attempt to prohibit or to restrain this execrable commerce. And that this assemblage of horrors might want no fact of distinguished die, he is now exciting those very people to rise in arms among us, and to purchase that liberty of which he has deprived them, by murdering the people upon whom he also obtruded them : thus paying off former crimes committed against the liberties of one people, with crimes which he urges them to commit against the lives of another.[78]

This grievance was removed at the insistence of the Southern states. The mere mention of the evils of slavery was enough to provoke them into disagreement.

Abolishing slavery in some of the Northern states was also contentious. In New York, it took the combined power of John Jay, Alexander Hamilton, and Aaron Burr fourteen years to pass the Act for the Gradual Abolition of Slavery. It would be nearly thirty more years before New York's last slaves received their freedom. If New York had such difficulty freeing its slaves, abolishing slavery in the South would be virtually impossible.

The real issue, however, was not whether the people wanted to free the slaves. Nearly everybody would have agreed to abolish slavery if it would have no economic or social costs. Most slaveholders would gladly have freed their slaves if they received adequate compensation and plans would be made to help the freed slave, such as providing them with some land to work. The issue was not whether to free the slaves, but who would bear the cost of doing so.

Freeing the slaves without compensating the slaveholders or helping the freed slaves become productive members of society would have destroyed the Southern economy. In 1774, slaves accounted for approximately 34 percent of the South's wealth and 21 percent of the entire country's wealth.[79] Depriving an entire region of a third of its wealth was impractical.

Southern slaveholders wanted the entire nation to pay for emancipation. James Madison argued, "It is the nation which is to reap the benefit. The nation therefore ought to bear the burden."[80] But Americans would never support a tax to compensate the slaveholders when they already opposed all attempts to raise taxes to pay down the debt or increase defense.

The North did not want to pay for what was seen by them to be a Southern problem. They also worried about the large influx of freed slaves coming north and causing economic and social upheaval. As a result, the South opposed emancipation while the North did not actively pursue it.

Despite opposition to emancipation in the South and only lackluster support in the North, historians continue to debate whether the Founding Fathers could have emancipated the slaves against the will of the general population. The question is whether the states would have ratified the Constitution if it abolished slavery.

A few years before the Constitutional Convention, Congress voted on a bill to abolish slavery as of 1800. Only six states voted for it.[81] When the issue of abolishing slavery was raised at the Constitutional Convention, Georgia and South Carolina threatened to withdraw. Some argue that the states in the Deep South would have had no choice but to join the new nation, even if the Constitution abolished slavery. Georgia unanimously ratified the Constitution because the new federal government would protect them from the Creek Indians and from the Spanish just across the border in Florida. Similarly, Edward Rutledge of South Carolina pointed out that his state must rely on "the naval force of our northern friends."[82] As a result, many argue that sparsely populated Southern states like South Carolina and Georgia—combined, they had less than six percent of the country's population—would have ratified the Constitution even if slavery had been abolished because they needed the defense the north provided. Additionally, they point out that the Union could have continued without those states.[83]

More likely, if the Constitution abolished slavery, South Carolina and Georgia would have waited to see what the larger Southern states did first. As it is, Virginia only ratified the Constitution by an 89 to 79 vote. Abolition of slavery could have pushed just enough delegates in Virginia's ratifying convention to vote against the Constitution. Without Virginia, the largest and most influential state, there likely would not have been a United States.

If Virginia had voted against the Constitution, South Carolina and Georgia would have seen things very differently. Most likely, the South would have begun talks to form their own union—one with slavery.

Not only did the Constitution fail to abolish slavery, it allowed for the importation of slaves for another twenty years and required the return of fugitive slaves. Again, South Carolina and Georgia threatened to oppose the Constitution if the importation of slaves was not allowed.[84] The fugitive slave clause, based on a similar provision in the Northwest Ordinance, passed unanimously and without debate.[85] That these provisions had to be included to garner the support of South Carolina and Georgia demonstrates how difficult it would have been to create a union including the South while abolishing slavery.

Despite its importance, the Constitutional Convention spent little time on the slavery issue. The delegates at the convention focused on the power of the states versus the federal government and the structure of the federal government. They were trying to create a new government with checks and balances, not remake American society.

Slavery was largely ignored at the Constitutional Convention in part because it was in decline at the time. Northern states were abolishing slavery on their own. Vermont eliminated slavery in 1777. New Hampshire and Massachusetts followed in 1783. Congress prohibited slavery in the Northwest Territory in 1787. Rhode Island, Connecticut, New York, New Jersey, and Pennsylvania would all enact laws gradually freeing their slaves.[86]

Manumission was also becoming increasingly popular in the South. In fact, there were more anti-slavery societies in the South than in the North. In Virginia, 13,000 slaves were freed in 1790, up from 3,000 ten years earlier.[87] With nearly 300,000 slaves in the state, almost half of the nation's total, Virginians were freeing about four percent of their slaves each year. At that rate, slavery would have disappeared completely within a generation or two. Already, one-eighth of blacks in Virginia were free.[88]

Slavery started disappearing in the South when Britain stopped buying tobacco from America during the war and imported from Turkey and Egypt instead, causing a decline in prices. Southern farmers switched production to other crops, most notably rice—the only industry in which slavery was still profitable. As Curtis Nettels writes in *The Emergence of a National Economy: 1775-1815*, "Immediately before 1792 slavery in the South was profitable only in the rice industry, and its scope there was extremely limited. If cotton had not spread over the lower South it is probable that slavery in the United States would have expired quickly or have declined to the point that its eventual abolition might have been effected without a disastrous national upheaval."[89]

The decline of slavery might have continued if not for the invention of the cotton gin in 1793. The South is inhospitable to the cleaner long-staple cotton because it requires a long growing season and sandy soil. Short-staple cotton, however, grows very well in the South, but its seeds were sticky and difficult to separate from the cotton fibers. Previously, it took twenty-five days to separate the seeds from one day's worth of cotton pickings. Eli Whitney's cotton gin reduced the time to remove the seeds to a single day.[90]

Cotton became a very profitable business in the Deep South after the invention of the cotton gin. As a result, cotton production exploded. Exports of cotton to England rose from nearly nothing to more than 15 million pounds in 1800 and was up to 48 million pounds by 1807, worth $11 million.[91] By 1860, cotton made up more than half of American exports.[92]

The market price of slaves rose along with demand, especially as slave productivity rose by more than 500 percent between 1810 and 1860.[93] The price of a slave in Charleston doubled between 1795 and 1804 and afterward remained stable for a number of years.[94] Between 1790 and 1860, Virginia and Maryland sold 835,000 slaves to the cotton-growing states farther south.[95] The United States imported tens of thousands of slaves before the federal government prohibited slave importation on January 1, 1808, though smuggling continued afterward. By 1810, there were more than a million slaves in the United States. The rate of growth in slavery between 1790 and 1810 was twice that of the 1775 to 1790 period.[96] The number of working slaves quadrupled between 1800 and 1860 to more than two million.[97]

Nevertheless, slavery's importance to the nation declined, though this was primarily because the North was growing faster than the South. The number of slaves declined from 16.9 percent of the total population in 1800 to 14.5 percent in 1840.[98]

However, slavery became more important to the South, especially to the Deep South. Slaves made up 18.4 percent of the population of the upcountry in South Carolina and Georgia in 1790. By 1820, that figure rose to 39.5 percent.[99]

In 1860, the value of slaves was greater than that of all the banks, factories, and railroads in the country.[100] Freeing all the slaves in 1860 and compensating the owners would have cost $2.7 billion. With a gross domestic product of $4.2 billion, the expense of this solution caused it to be ignored. However, the Civil War cost about $6.6 billion, so compensating the slaveholders would have been much cheaper than going to war.[101] But nobody in 1787 or even in 1860 knew how long, brutal, and costly the Civil War would be.

By increasing the value of the slaves and concentrating them in the Deep South, the cotton gin made complete emancipation a much more difficult proposition than it would have been in 1787. However, there was no way for the delegates to the Constitutional Convention to foresee this radical change. The Constitutional Convention saw little reason to risk everything when slavery was disappearing on its own as the importance of tobacco, indigo, and rice declined and slavery became less profitable. Additionally, the world and the nation were industrializing. The economy was shifting away from manual labor and moving toward increased use of capital and the skilled labor required to design, build, operate, and maintain such machinery. Letting slavery slowly fade away was a logical choice and one that would assist the accomplishment of the Founding Fathers' primary goal—the ratification of the Constitution.

Assuming the delegates at the Constitutional Convention abolished slavery and the Constitution was still ratified by all the states, there is no guarantee that conditions for the blacks would have improved in any significant manner. The South would have done all it could to keep its social and economic systems, especially after the invention of the cotton gin. Just as freed slaves became serf-like sharecroppers after the Civil War, the same would likely have occurred if slavery had been abolished in the Constitution. Just as it took more than one hundred years for blacks to achieve equality in the South after the Civil War, there is little reason to believe blacks would have achieved equality if slavery had been abolished in 1787.

Already, there were ongoing conflicts between whites and free blacks in the North in the late 1700s and early 1800s, most notably in Philadelphia.[102] If the North had trouble living side-by-side with free blacks, it would have been much worse in the South, as it was for about a century after the Civil War.

In many respects, the United States was already leading the way to the abolition of slavery. Vermont was the first state in the history of the world to eliminate slavery through legislation in 1777 and the other Northern states followed shortly thereafter. By comparison, Britain had been proslavery in its colonial possessions up through the early 1800s. Only after the American Revolution, when Britain had lost some of its possessions and slavery became less vital to the Empire, did they begin moving toward more emancipatory policies.[103] While slavery in England and Wales was determined to be illegal in 1772 by William Murray, First Earl of Mansfield, this ruling was largely ignored. The Slave Trade Act of 1807 outlawed the slave trade in the British Empire, less than a year before the United States' 1808 ban on slave importation went into effect. However, every state except for South Carolina banned the importation of slaves from Africa even before the federal ban of 1808.[104]

In fact, most European countries banned the slave trade around the same time as Britain and the United States. Denmark eliminated slave trading in 1804, Sweden did so in 1813, France in 1818, and Spain outlawed it in 1820. However, in these countries, as in the United States and Britain, enforcement was lax.[105] Considering these European countries had far fewer slaves within their home countries, the abolition of slavery was much easier to accomplish in Europe where economic losses and social upheaval were minimal. Furthermore, when Britain finally emancipated its slaves in 1833, the government compensated the slaveholders, something that would have been much more costly in the United States.

Even though Britain's Slavery Abolition Act of 1833 preceded Abraham Lincoln's Emancipation Proclamation by thirty years, it came more than half a century after America's Northern states started abolishing slavery. As a whole, the United States was slower in the emancipation of slaves than the Europeans, but many American states were quicker to do so. Given the South's reliance on slavery compared with that of Britain and the other European countries, the abolition of slavery in the United States was much more difficult and a much greater sacrifice by those people and states who voluntarily freed their slaves.

Furthermore, slavery in United States was just a small part of the international problem. Less than ten percent of all slaves shipped to the New World in the eighteenth century came to the thirteen colonies.[106] Abolishing slavery in the United States would have done nothing for the other ninety percent. However, by advancing the cause of liberty, the Founding Fathers established an environment in which the institution of slavery could be attacked. Gordon Wood writes in *The American Revolution: A History*, "The Revolution had a powerful effect in eventually bringing an end to slavery in America. It suddenly and effectively ended the social and intellectual environment that had allowed slavery to exist everywhere for thousands of years without substantial questioning."[107] Just as the American Revolution instigated struggles for liberty around the world, the revolution called slavery into question wherever it existed.

The Founding Fathers were aware that, even if they could not abolish slavery, they could lay the groundwork for its eradication. The Founders refused to include the words *slave* and *slavery* in the Constitution because, as Madison argued, it would be "wrong to admit in the Constitution the idea that there could be property in men."[108]

Frederick Douglass, an escaped slave and leading abolitionist, said, "Interpreted, as it ought to be interpreted, the Constitution is a glorious liberty document... Take the Constitution according to its plain reading, and I defy the presentation of a single pro-slavery clause in it. On the other hand it will be found to contain principles and purposes, entirely hostile to the existence of slavery."[109] The Founding Fathers could not abolish slavery, but they created a Constitution that was "entirely hostile" to its existence. At a time when slavery was accepted throughout the world, this was a remarkable achievement.

Although many of the Founding Fathers tried to achieve emancipation for the slaves, these Founding Fathers were quite busy establishing a new nation. Unfortunately for hundreds of thousands of slaves in America, the Founders could not do much to help them. The Founding Fathers recognized that they would have to *sacrifice* the slaves to get their republic. James Madison, for one, opposed slavery in theory, but realized it was "a peculiar" case and said that allowing slavery to exist in the new republic was "the compromising expedient of the Constitution."[110] The Founding Fathers knew the Constitution would not be perfect, though they hoped it would be the best constitution ever written. Slavery was one flaw they had to accept to establish their new republic.

The Founding Fathers were ideologues, but they were also practical, both in creating a union and maintaining the economy. Writing a constitution that abolished slavery, but having it fail in the ratifying conventions, would not have helped the slaves. If ratifying a constitution that abolished slavery were possible, there is no knowing what economic and social turmoil it would have caused. That turmoil would have made it easier for America's enemies to invade, especially with the United States already in border disputes with Spain and Britain.

The Founding Fathers did all they could to help the slaves without compromising the Constitution. Through the Constitution, the Founding Fathers enabled the states to free the slaves, as many states did, and also enabled the federal government to restrict slavery in certain ways, which the government did in 1808 when it banned the importation of slaves. Their opposition to slavery is noteworthy in an age when it was commonly accepted. That they failed to abolish slavery is not because they lacked morals or courage, but because the people were not yet ready for abolition. In democracies—and the states were still very democratic—only the people can enact laws. The Founding Fathers needed the consent of the governed and the abolition of slavery almost certainly would have meant the failure to ratify the Constitution.

THE RATIFICATION DEBATE

Congress forwarded the proposed constitution to special state conventions for approval. To go into effect, nine states had to ratify the Constitution, though its supporters wanted all thirteen states to join the

Union. Additionally, there were certain states that, for all practical purposes, had to ratify it for the nation to come together. If a big state like New York, Pennsylvania, or Virginia voted against it, the Union stood little chance of surviving. However, if a small state like Rhode Island voted against it, this would be of little consequence and the Union could be formed without that state.

Ratification was anything but assured and the big stumbling block was not slavery. Instead, the major impediments were the lack of a bill of rights, the question of whether the large states or small states would dominate, and concerns over the power of the federal government versus the state governments. As a result, the ratification battle took longer and was more contentious than the drafting of the Constitution.

Three delegates to the Constitutional Convention refused to endorse the Constitution. George Mason attended the convention and was the fifth most frequent speaker, but opposed the Constitution because it lacked a bill of rights. He was an outspoken opponent during the ratification debate. Elbridge Gerry also opposed the Constitution because it lacked a bill of rights and led the opposition to it in Massachusetts. Edmund Randolph also refused to sign the Constitution because he thought it lacked sufficient checks and balances and he wanted to make further changes, but then voted for ratification in the Virginia Ratifying Convention because he thought the Constitution superior to the Articles of Confederation. Another thirteen delegates left the Constitutional Convention early, but most of these men departed for personal reasons and supported ratification. However, Robert Yates, John Lansing, Luther Martin, and John Mercer left the convention early and opposed ratification.

Thomas Jefferson, who was in Paris at the time, was unsure about the Constitution. Jefferson supported the convention and called the delegates "an assembly of demigods,"[111] but he opposed their meeting behind closed doors. Upon seeing the finished product, Jefferson said, "There are very good articles in it: and very bad. I do not know which preponderate."[112] Jefferson suggested that nine states ratify the Constitution, but that four withhold their approval until a bill of rights could be drafted and approved.[113] Additionally, there were those who refused to attend the Constitutional Convention from the outset. Patrick Henry disapproved of the convention and refused to attend, announcing "I smell a rat!"

Throughout the colonies, the Anti-Federalists fought against this proposed constitution or fought to have it amended and resubmitted. While the Federalists thought the system of dual sovereignty was essential because the federal and state governments would be able to check each other, some Anti-Federalists did not believe that the state and federal governments could coexist. Writing as Agrippa in the Massachusetts Gazette, John Winthrop argued, "We shall find it impossible to please two masters."[114] Additionally, the lack of a bill of rights concerned many Anti-Federalists. When the Federalists agreed to add a bill of rights once the new government was established, a number of Anti-Federalists became outright supporters of the new Constitution.[115] Without that promise, the Constitution would have gone down in defeat.

The large states proved to be another obstacle to ratification. They were reluctant to give up their power to a national government because they believed that they could succeed on their own. The small states would more greatly benefit from a shared defense and unrestricted interstate commerce and most of them quickly ratified the Constitution by large margins. As a result, the most contentious battles over ratification occurred in the large states of New York and Virginia. To convince them that they would benefit greatly from a stronger national union, Alexander Hamilton, John Jay, and James Madison wrote eighty-five essays under the pseudonym Publius—the Federalist Papers—explaining the Constitution.

Despite the months of effort in Philadelphia, the support of many of America's most prominent leaders, and the arguments set forth in the Federalist Papers, the Constitution almost failed to get ratified. The ratification process went smoothly at first, part of the Federalists' momentum-building strategy. In the months of December 1787 and January 1788, Delaware, New Jersey, and Georgia unanimously ratified the Constitution, Connecticut approved it by a three-to-one margin, and Pennsylvania by a two-to-one margin. In a span of just thirty-three days, five of the nine requisite states easily ratified the Constitution.

Then the process slowed down. In February, Massachusetts just barely ratified the Constitution by a 187 to 168 vote. Had Massachusetts rejected it, the grand experiment could have ended because other states might have followed this important state's lead. In March, Rhode Island rejected the Constitution in a popular referendum by a vote of 2,708 to 237 because it lacked a bill of rights.

In April, Maryland ratified it by a nearly six-to-one margin. In May, South Carolina voted two to one in favor of the Constitution. New Hampshire became the ninth state when it ratified the Constitution by a 57 to 47 vote in June. Nine states had joined the new constitutional republic, but it still lacked two of the most important states: New York and Virginia. Without these two states, the country would be divided with New York separating New England from the middle states and Virginia separating the middle states from the South.

Madison led the charge for ratification in Virginia while Hamilton did the same in New York. With George Washington supporting ratification, Virginia ratified it by a narrow 89 to 79 margin in June 1788. With 10 of the 13 states already ratifying the Constitution, the arguments set forth in the Federalist Papers, and Hamilton's hard work at the state's ratifying convention, New York somewhat reluctantly ratified it by a 30 to 27 margin, even though New York's powerful governor, George Clinton, opposed ratification.

When the United States of America began operating in March 1789, it had just 11 states. North Carolina did not ratify the Constitution until November 1789, though it did so by an overwhelming 194 to 77 vote. Back in August 1788, North Carolina voted to adjourn, neither ratifying nor rejecting the Constitution outright, demanding a bill of rights first. Rhode Island would not join the union until May 1790 and ratified the Constitution by a vote of just 34 to 32.[116]

With so many close votes, one rejection, and one adjournment, the battle over ratification was intense. Between November 14, 1787 and April 2, 1788, Hamilton wrote forty-two Federalist Papers, Madison penned twenty-nine, and Jay added one—a total of seventy-two of the eighty-five essays. Each week for four and a half months, three or four new Federalist Papers, on average, appeared in dozens of newspapers around the country. In fact, some subscribers pleaded with their newspapers to stop "cramming us with the voluminous PUBLIUS."[117]

These were not just any essays. George Washington said that the Federalist Papers "have thrown new light upon the science of government" and "cannot fail to make a lasting impression upon those, who read the best publications on the subject."[118] Thomas Jefferson called them "the best commentary on the principles of government, which ever was written." Jefferson even admitted, "it has rectified me on several points," though he continued to insist on the necessity of a bill of rights.[119] In 1807, Supreme Court Justice John Marshall predicted that the Federalist Papers "will be read and admired when the controversy in which that valuable treatise on government originated, shall be no longer remembered."[120]

Not that the Anti-Federalists sat aside and did nothing during this debate. The Anti-Federalists wrote their own essays, making some strong arguments against the Constitution. However, the Anti-Federalists did not propose a comprehensive alternative. Just as the angry mobs protested and created chaos without offering feasible solutions, the Anti-Federalists had complaints but few solutions. Their answer was to stick with the Articles of Confederation and make some minor improvements. In the end, the people supported the Constitution for the lack of any better proposal.

Furthermore, the Anti-Federalists were disorganized in their attack on the Constitution. Some Anti-Federalists opposed the Constitution because it lacked a bill of rights, then switched sides or removed themselves from the debate when the Federalists promised to add one after the Constitution was ratified. Some opposed it because it allowed slavery, but others opposed it because it did not protect slavery sufficiently and would enable Congress to abolish the slave trade after twenty years. Some Anti-Federalists argued that the Senate would control the President because of its power to impeach and its power to approve or reject treaties. Others said the new system would lead to monarchy. The Anti-Federalists were attacking from all fronts, but they were disorganized.

The Anti-Federalists also got desperate. Some opponents of the Constitution even attacked George Washington's "unsuspected goodness and zeal" and Benjamin Franklin's "weakness and indecision attendant on old age."[121] When John Jay stopped writing Federalist Papers after authoring just four in October and November 1787, the Anti-Federalists spread rumors that he had changed his mind and opposed the Constitution. In reality, Jay had rheumatoid arthritis and could not write. Jay would author one more Federalist Paper in March 1788, but was severely injured in April 1788 defending innocent doctors against an angry mob in an incident known as the Doctors' Riot. This prevented him from writing more Federalist Papers, though he managed to attend the New York Ratifying Convention that began in June 1788.

In Federalist No. 28, James Madison wrote about the haphazard nature of the Anti-Federalists' arguments:

> This one tells us that the proposed Constitution ought to be rejected, because it is not a confederation of the States, but a government over individuals. Another admits that it ought to be a government over individuals to a certain extent, but by no means to the extent proposed. A third does not object to the government over individuals, or to the extent proposed, but to the want of a bill of rights. A fourth concurs in the absolute necessity of a bill of rights, but contends that it ought to be declaratory, not of the personal rights of individuals, but of the rights reserved to the States in their political capacity. A fifth is of opinion that a bill of rights of any sort would be superfluous and misplaced, and that the plan would be unexceptionable but for the fatal power of regulating the times and places of election... It is a matter both of wonder and regret, that those who raise so many objections against the new Constitution should never call to mind the defects of that which is to be exchanged for it. It is not necessary that the former should be perfect; it is sufficient that the latter is more imperfect.

Whereas the Anti-Federalists were disorganized, engaged in personal attacks, and offered few solutions, the Federalists were extremely well organized and prepared for this debate. The Federalist Papers of Hamilton and Madison built upon the research they had done prior to the Constitutional Convention and on the debates within it.[122] Whereas the Federalists were ready to defend the Constitution right away, the Anti-Federalists were only able to start analyzing the Constitution and develop counterarguments after the Constitutional Convention was completed and the text of the Constitution became public.

The Federalists were better able to coordinate their actions and arguments because many of them had served together in the Army, Congress, and Constitutional Convention. They had far greater influence among the people because they were national and even international heroes and celebrities. In contrast, the Anti-Federalists, by their very nature, focused primarily on state and local issues and few were known outside of their own states. While historians may argue about which group was smarter, which side wrote better essays, and which was more prescient about the future of the United States, the organization and fame of the Federalists enabled them to win this political battle.

The Federalists also had the newspapers on their side. Of the nation's ninety-two newspapers and magazines, only twelve supported the Anti-Federalist cause.[123] Alexander Hamilton used his connections to have four of the five New York City newspapers publish the Federalist Papers.[124] This access to the media was essential to winning the ratification debate, especially in swing states like New York.

In his American history book, *Give Me Liberty!*, Eric Foner writes, "In the end, the supporters' energy and organization, coupled with their domination of the colonial press, carried the day."[125] Their organization and influence helped the Federalists deliver their message to the people, but they still needed a strong message to deliver. The Federalist Papers provided that clear but powerful message.

The strongest argument for ratification, however, was made by the situation in the states. The dismal condition of the nation under the Articles of Confederation compelled the people to adopt the Constitution. As Hamilton stated at the Constitutional Convention, "The people are gradually ripening in their opinions of government; they begin to be tired of an excess of democracy."[126] In the end, all the states, even those that had their doubts, ratified the Constitution because they saw that the alternatives—thirteen separate nations, continuing under the Articles of Confederation, or summoning a new convention to rewrite or amend the proposed constitution—were almost certainly worse than what the Founding Fathers had offered them.

Nevertheless, ratification was a difficult battle that the Founding Fathers almost lost. This was the strength of the supporters of state and local democracy. It took the combined will of the greatest collection of men in history, the "assembly of demigods," to just barely win this political battle.

SUCCESS

With the ratification of the Constitution, the Founding Fathers replaced the Articles of Confederation with their grand experiment in republican government. However, the Founding Fathers did not dictatorially impose their new government on the people. They simply recommended the Constitution to Congress and requested that Congress forward it to state ratifying conventions. Nine of the thirteen states had to ratify the Constitution for it to go into effect and it would not be binding on those states that voted against it. The Founding Fathers merely recommended a new form of government, which required the approval of Congress and the consent of the people. The Founding Fathers led a legal, peaceful, and bloodless revolution. And the people approved.

The Constitution fixed virtually all the flaws of the Articles of Confederation. The new national government received the power to tax, coin money, and negotiate treaties with foreign nations. The Constitution eliminated interstate tariffs, thereby creating a giant free trade zone, a "great American system" as Hamilton called it.[127]

The Constitution restrained the state governments. Many powers were taken away from the state governments and given to the federal government, which the Founders hoped would be better managed. Alexis de Tocqueville confirms that the Founding Fathers were wise to place their trust in the new federal government rather than the states: "The business of the Union is, for any attentive observer, infinitely better managed than the business of any individual state. The federal government is more equitable and temperate in its proceedings than that of the states. There is more wisdom in its outlook; its projects are planned further ahead and more skillfully; its measures are executed with more aptitude, consistency, and firmness."[128]

The resulting Constitution was nearly perfect. It divided power among the people, states, and federal government. It created checks and balances between the executive, legislative, and judicial branches. No constitution of this kind had ever been created before. None has since exceeded it.

Nevertheless, perfection is impossible. The Founding Fathers did not expect their Constitution to be perfect because, as George Washington said, "We are not to expect perfection in this world."[129] The Constitution came close, though.

On September 17, 1787, just prior to the signing of the Constitution, James Wilson presented to the Constitutional Convention a speech written by Benjamin Franklin. Franklin had written, "It therefore astonishes me, Sir, to find this system approaching so near to perfection as it does... Thus I consent, Sir, to this Constitution because I expect no better, and because I am not sure, that it is not the best."[130]

James Wilson himself said, "I am satisfied that anything nearer to perfection could not have been accomplished... I am bold to assert that it is the best form of government which has ever been offered to the world."[131] George Washington concurred, "I was convinced it approached nearer to perfection than any government hitherto instituted among Men."[132]

Alexander Hamilton also agreed, "The system, though it may not be perfect in every part, is, upon the whole, a good one; is the best that the present views and circumstances of the country will permit." Hamilton continued that he would not "expose the Union to the jeopardy of successive experiments, in the chimerical pursuit of a perfect plan. I never expect to see a perfect work from imperfect man."[133]

Hamilton added that the Constitution, though imperfect, would lead to perfection: "There are two objects in forming systems of government—safety for the people, and energy in the administration... Good constitutions are formed upon a comparison of the liberty of the individual with the strength of the government... Through the opposition and mutual control of these bodies, the government will reach, in its operations, the perfect balance between liberty and power."[134]

If "the Revolution was in the minds and hearts of the people," as John Adams argued,[135] then the Constitution was even more revolutionary than defeating Britain and winning independence. James Madison wrote about the creators of the Constitution: "They accomplished a revolution which has no parallel in the annals of human society. They reared the fabrics of governments which have no model on the face of the globe. They formed the design of a great Confederacy, which it is incumbent on their successors to improve and perpetuate."[136]

Unlike the War for Independence, this revolution did not require years of fighting and thousands of deaths. It was accomplished by studying political philosophy, thoughtful deliberation, and compromise. James Wilson wrote, "After a period of six thousand years has elapsed since the creation, the United States exhibit to the world the first instance, as far as we can learn, of a nation, unattacked by external force, unconvulsed by domestic insurrections, assembling voluntarily, deliberating fully, and deciding calmly, concerning that system of government, under which they would wish that they and their posterity should live."[137]

Thomas Jefferson wrote, "The example of changing a constitution, by assembling the wise men of the State, instead of assembling armies, will be worth as much to the world as the former examples we had given them. The Constitution, too, which was the result of our deliberations, is unquestionably the wisest ever yet presented to men."[138]

John Jay wrote, "The Americans are the first people whom Heaven has favored with an opportunity of deliberating upon, and choosing the forms of government under which they should live; all other constitutions have derived their existence from violence or accidental circumstances, and are therefore probably more distant from their perfection, which though beyond our reach, may nevertheless be approached under the guidance of reason and experience."[139]

John Adams called the Constitution "the greatest single effort of national deliberation the world had ever seen."[140] Daniel Webster said, "We live under the only government that ever existed which was framed by the unrestrained and deliberate consultations of the people."[141] William Gladstone, the four-time British Prime Minister, called the Constitution "the most remarkable work known to me in modern times to have been produced by the human intellect."[142]

Most governments in ancient history, including those of Athens and Sparta, were established "by some individual citizen of preeminent wisdom and approved integrity."[143] The Founding Fathers, however, designed their government as a group, just as Montesquieu recommended in *The Spirit of Laws*, where he wrote, "whatever depends on the legislative power is oftentimes better regulated by many than by a single person."[144]

In contrast, the Roman constitution was largely the result of trial and error. Polybius writes, "The Romans while they have arrived at the same final result as regards their form of government, have not reached it by any process of reasoning, but by the discipline of many struggles and troubles, and always choosing the best by the light of the experience gained in disaster have thus reached…the best of all existing constitutions."[145] But the Founding Fathers did not have time to experiment with governmental systems. They had to act quickly to save the American Revolution. As Hamilton wrote, the Founders had to see "whether societies of men are really capable or not of establishing good government from reflection and choice, or whether they are forever destined to depend for their political constitutions on accident and force."[146] Fortunately, the Founding Fathers studied the history and governments of ancient Greece, ancient Rome, Britain, and the states. They had the writings of Aristotle, Plato, Polybius, Plutarch, Locke, Montesquieu, and many others to follow.[147]

Additionally, America and the Founding Fathers had God on their side. Many Founding Fathers argued that the odds against the Constitutional Convention were so great that the creation of the Constitution could have occurred only with the help of God. When Benjamin Rush, a signer of the Declaration of Independence, considered the Constitution and how it was created, "he fairly deduced it from heaven, asserting that he as much believed the hand of God was employed in this work, as that God had divided the Red Sea to give a passage to the children of Israel, or had fulminated the ten commandments from Mount Sinai."[148]

In fact, the Founding Fathers believed that the entire American Revolution—from the war against Britain to the writing of the Constitution—

was a long series of miraculous events. In Washington's first inaugural address, he declared, "No People can be bound to acknowledge and adore the invisible hand, which conducts the Affairs of men more than the People of the United States. Every step, by which they have advanced to the character of an independent nation, seems to have been distinguished by some token of providential agency."[149]

James Madison also attributed the success of the American Revolution to God. He wrote in the Federalist Papers, "It is impossible for any man of candor to reflect on this circumstance without partaking of the astonishment. It is impossible for the man of pious reflection not to perceive in it a finger of that Almighty hand which has been so frequently and signally extended to our relief in the critical stages of the revolution."[150] Years later, Madison wrote, "The happy Union of these States is a wonder; their Constitution a miracle."[151]

The Founding Fathers believed that the American Revolution and the Constitution in particular would change not just America, but the entire world for the better. As Thomas Paine wrote in *Common Sense*, "We have it in our power to begin the world over again. A situation similar to the present, hath not happened since the days of Noah."[152] Alexander Hamilton also believed it was up to America "to vindicate the honor of the human race."[153] He argued for the Constitution because not doing so may "deserve to be considered as the general misfortune of mankind."[154]

Madison concurred, "Happily for America, happily, we trust, for the whole human race, they pursued a new and more noble course... To this manly spirit, posterity will be indebted for the possession, and the world for the example, of the numerous innovations displayed on the American theatre, in favor of private rights and public happiness."[155] Madison added that the United States and its Constitution should be "the hope of Liberty throughout the world."[156]

Similarly, in his First Inaugural Address in 1801, Thomas Jefferson called the United States government "the world's best hope."[157] That same year, he wrote to John Dickinson, "A just and solid republican government maintained here, will be a standing monument & example for the aim & imitation of the people of other countries; and I join with you in the hope and belief that they will see, from our example, that a free government is of all others the most energetic; that the inquiry which has been excited among the mass of mankind by our revolution & its consequences, will ameliorate the condition of man over a great portion of the globe."[158]

The following year, in a Fourth of July oration, Daniel Webster admonished the people to protect and defend their Constitution, for not only does their own safety and happiness depend on it, but also that of the entire world. "Miracles to not cluster. That which has happened but once in six thousand years cannot be expected to happen often. Such a government, once gone, might leave a void, to be filled, for ages, with revolution and tumult, riot and despotism. The history of the world is before it."[159]

The Constitution was revolutionary, a miracle, and "the world's best hope."[160] But its success was not assured. The Founders realized that no piece of paper could effectively prevent tyranny and promote liberty. It needs the people's support.

Nevertheless, the future looked promising for the United States. Benjamin Franklin pointed out, "Our new Constitution is now established, and has an appearance that promises permanency; but in the world nothing can be said to be certain, except death and taxes."[161] It would be up to the Founding Fathers to lead the nation to success and "permanency" in the years to follow.

CHAPTER SIX

A REPUBLIC, IF YOU CAN KEEP IT.

A fter the Constitutional Convention, a lady reportedly asked Benjamin Franklin, "Well, Doctor, what have we got—a Republic or a Monarchy?" Franklin replied, "A Republic, if you can keep it."[1] Although the Founding Fathers believed republican forms of government were best, constant vigilance is still required to maintain them.

Many of the issues so hotly debated and contested in colonial America, during the war, and under the Articles of Confederation remained in the forefront in the new republic. The "balance between liberty and power,"[2] the size of government, the balance of power between the states and federal government, the monetary system, westward expansion, and taxes would all be major points of contention in the next few decades. The battle raged on between the angry mobs, who wanted democracy and unlimited liberty, and the Founding Fathers, who wanted law and order.

The Constitution provided the blueprint for the United States, but the new government still had to be built. The United States had no tax system, no public credit, no monetary system, and huge debts to pay off.[3]

Yet again, the Founding Fathers would provide the much-needed leadership at this critical moment. Whereas the revolution of the angry mobs led to chaos under the Confederation government, the revolution of the Founding Fathers led to political stability, prosperity, and tranquility.

FEDERALISTS AND REPUBLICANS

The Founding Fathers who wrote and supported the Constitution called themselves Federalists. Led by George Washington and Alexander Hamilton, the Federalists supported a limited but active federal government. After the experience under the Articles of Confederation, they believed that some political power should be taken away from the states and given to the national government. The total power of government would remain unchanged, but the balance would shift toward the federal government. That was a major purpose of the Constitution and the Federalists continued to pursue that goal in the new government. As the federal government took over defense and banking, for example, the activity of the states in those fields declined or disappeared entirely.

In contrast, the Anti-Federalists opposed the Constitution. They wanted to protect the rights of the people and maintain the power of the states. They wanted to give the federal government even less power than the Constitution had assigned it.

These Anti-Federalists, along with Thomas Jefferson, James Madison, and others, became the Republicans. Although Thomas Jefferson was never an Anti-Federalist, he was never a Federalist either. Jefferson sympathized with the Anti-Federalist cause and only half-heartedly supported the Constitution during the ratification debate. For his part, James Madison left the Federalist camp and helped found the Republican Party. "Republican federalists" is what Jefferson called men like Madison who supported the Constitution but opposed what they saw as an increasingly powerful federal government.[4]

Whereas the Federalists feared the tyranny of the states, the Anti-Federalists feared the tyranny of the federal government. As is evident from the Federalist and Anti-Federalist Papers, both sides favored limited government. The argument between them was not necessarily over the size of government, but how best to balance the power of the states and federal government.

While the Federalists supported the Constitution they created, the Republicans rallied around the Declaration of Independence that Jefferson had authored. The Anti-Federalists, and the Republicans to a smaller degree, argued that the Federalists had abandoned the principles of the revolution as set forth by the Declaration of Independence. The political landscape of the 1790s became a battle between "the spirit of '76" supporting the Declaration of Independence and "the spirit of '87" supporting the Constitution.[5]

Throughout the 1790s, these two camps fought for the votes of the people and, thereby, control of the government. The Republicans and Federalists opposed each other on every major issue, including taxes, assumption of state debt, banking, foreign affairs, and land sales in the West.

BILL OF RIGHTS

The first major issue faced by the new government was the addition of a bill of rights to the Constitution. The Federalists had some objections to a bill of rights. They pointed out that the Articles of Confederation and four state constitutions lacked bills of rights, including that of New York, home of leading Anti-Federalist George Clinton, even though the states had been acting as independent republics for years.[6] However, the Federalists promised the Anti-Federalists that they would add a bill of rights in exchange for their votes in favor of ratification. Therefore, the Federalists did not oppose a bill of rights, but did not promote it either.

The Federalists believed that a bill of rights was unnecessary because those rights were already protected by the Constitution, even if they were not specifically listed.[7] Madison wrote in Federalist No. 45, "The powers delegated by the proposed Constitution to the federal government are few and defined." If the federal government's powers were few and defined, it could not infringe on the rights of the people. If the government were to go beyond its limited powers and the checks in the Constitution proved insufficient to halt this abuse, a bill of rights would have little effect.

One concern that the Founding Fathers had with bills of rights is that any list of "declaratory and restrictive clauses"[8] could not possibly contain all the rights belonging to the people. Alexander Hamilton argued, "I go further, and affirm that bills of rights, in the sense and to the extent in which they are contended for, are not only unnecessary in the proposed Constitution, but would even be dangerous. They would contain various exceptions to powers not granted; and, on this very account, would afford a colorable pretext to claim more than were granted. For why declare that things shall not be done which there is no power to do?"[9]

Even though James Madison authored the Bill of Rights and introduced it in the House of Representatives, he had mixed feelings toward bills of rights. Madison wrote to Jefferson, "There are many who think such addition unnecessary, and not a few who think it misplaced in such a Constitution... My own opinion has always been in favor of a bill of rights... At the same time I have never thought the omission a material defect... I have not viewed it in an important light." Madison then listed four reasons a bill of rights was not needed, among these "because the limited powers of the federal Government and the jealousy of the subordinate Governments, afford a security" and "experience proves the inefficacy of a bill of rights on those occasions when its controul is most needed."[10]

To counter some of these arguments, Madison included the Ninth Amendment:

> The enumeration in the Constitution, of certain rights, shall not be construed to deny or disparage others retained by the people.

Madison admitted that he designed the Ninth Amendment to protect against the arguments he and Hamilton made against bills of rights. Upon introducing the Bill of Rights, Madison said, "It has been objected also against a bill of rights, that, by enumerating particular exceptions to the grant of power, it would disparage those rights which were not placed in that enumeration; and it might follow by implication, that those rights which were not singled out, were intended to be assigned into the hands of the General Government, and were consequently insecure. This is one of the most plausible arguments I have ever heard urged against the admission of a bill of rights into this system; but, I conceive, that it may be guarded against. I have attempted it."[11]

Despite the ardent demands of the Anti-Federalists, nobody seemed to be in any rush to enact the Bill of Rights. This issue was only brought up at the very end of the Constitutional Convention. It took more than two years to get the Bill of Rights ratified whereas it took only nine months to ratify the Constitution. Three of the original thirteen states—Connecticut, Georgia, and Massachusetts—failed to ratify the Bill of Rights until 1939. The popular support for the Bill of Rights, or at least the urgency, was lower than it had been for the Constitution.

THE AMERICAN ECONOMIC SYSTEM

The Constitution gave the national government financial powers that it lacked under the Articles of Confederation. The federal government received the power "To lay and collect Taxes, Duties, Imposts and Excises," "To borrow money on the credit of the United States," and "To coin Money, regulate the Value thereof, and of foreign Coin, and fix the Standard of Weights and Measures."[12]

Although the federal government's power is limited to the Constitution's enumerated powers, the government also has certain implied powers under the "necessary and proper" clause of the Constitution. As James Madison argued, "Had the convention attempted a positive enumeration of the powers necessary and proper for carrying their other powers into effect, the attempt would have involved a complete digest of laws on every subject to which the Constitution relates... Had they attempted to enumerate the particular powers or means not necessary or proper for carrying the general powers into execution, the task would have been no less chimerical... No axiom is more clearly established in law, or in reason, than that wherever the end is required, the means are authorized; wherever a general power to do a thing is given, every particular power necessary for doing it is included."[13] Much of the debate in the 1790s revolved around these two issues: the federal government's power in financial matters and the nature of these implied powers.

President George Washington appointed Alexander Hamilton to the position of Secretary of the Treasury. At the time, there was no United States economy. Instead, there were thirteen different economies, each with its own tariffs and money. Hamilton's job was to create a national economy, establish a stream of revenue for the government, fund the debt, establish credit, and create a stable currency.

The Founding Fathers believed that nothing was more important than paying off the debt. In 1792, George Washington said, "No measure can be more desirable, whether viewed with an eye to its intrinsic importance, or to the general sentiment and wish of the Nation" than to establish "a systematic and effectual arrangement for the regular redemption and discharge of the public debt."[14] A year later, Washington added, "No pecuniary consideration is more urgent than the regular redemption and discharge of the public debt."[15] Similarly, Thomas Jefferson wrote, "I, however, place economy among the first and most important republican virtues, and public debt as the greatest of the dangers to be feared."[16] Funding the debt would also help the United States develop a solid credit rating.

To fund the debt and run the government, new taxes needed to be imposed, even though the people would certainly resist them, just as they had resisted new taxes for the previous thirty years. The federal government had three possible methods of generating revenue: consumption taxes known as excise taxes, import taxes known as tariffs, and land sales. Revenue from land sales would be extremely volatile, rising and falling more sharply than excise taxes or tariffs as the economy expands and contracts. Excise taxes would require voluntary payment or an army of tax collectors. Tariffs, though, were relatively easy to collect because they only required customs officers at ports of entry. As an additional benefit, tariffs would encourage domestic industry.[17] As a result, for most of the pre-Civil War period, tariffs generated over eighty percent of the federal government's revenue.[18]

In 1789, Alexander Hamilton proposed a tariff of 5 percent on most imports. Thirty enumerated goods had higher rates averaging 8 percent with luxury items taxed at a rate of up to 15 percent.[19] Additionally, the Tonnage Act of 1789 charged a duty of 50 cents per ton on foreign ships, 30 cents per ton on American-built ships owned by foreigners, and 6 cents per ton on ships owned and built by Americans.[20]

Although Jefferson and Madison would later argue against protective tariffs, these tariffs were not strongly opposed.[21] Jefferson was still overseas when Congress passed these bills. Madison supported the Tariff and Tonnage Acts. Like Hamilton, Madison wanted a strong shipping industry to help train men for the navy. Additionally, Madison thought these acts might pressure Britain into opening the West Indies to American shipping. Furthermore, Madison wanted to promote American industry by raising the cost of British goods. However, Madison thought that the higher tariff rates should have applied to a different list of items.[22]

With revenue to fund the debt, Hamilton proposed that all the government's debts be paid at full face value, all payments be made to the current holders of the debt, and that all state debts be assumed by the federal government. Hamilton argued that these steps were necessary "for the support of public credit" and to "promote the increasing respectability of the American name; to answer the calls of justice; to restore landed property to its due value; to furnish new resources both to agriculture and commerce; to cement more closely the union of the states; to add to their security against foreign attack; to establish public order on the basis of an upright and liberal policy."[23] Hamilton also wanted to "make it the immediate interest of the moneyed men to cooperate with Government in its support."[24]

Hamilton's recommendation that all debts be paid at face value saw little opposition. Although the Constitution clearly states that "All Debts contracted and Engagements entered into, before the Adoption of this Constitution, shall be as valid against the United States under this Constitution, as under the Confederation," there was some debate whether the new government would redeem the debt at its full value or at the current market value. Nevertheless, most agreed that the debt should be redeemed at its full value.

However, the question of debt discrimination faced more opposition. For years, the government had paid soldiers and suppliers with government bonds. Many of these people sold their bonds to speculators, receiving just a fraction of their original face value. The Republicans thought that the original holders of the debt, not the speculators, should receive the full value. Hamilton and the Federalists argued that doing so would be a "breach of contract" because "the nature of the contract, in its origin, is, that the public will pay the sum expressed in the security, to the first holder or his assignee." Hamilton further explained, "The intent in making the security assignable, is, that the proprietor may be able to make use of his property, by selling it for as much as it may be worth in the market, and that the buyer may be safe in the purchase."[25]

In the House of Representatives, James Madison proposed paying the original holders instead of the current owners of the securities, but his bill was easily defeated. Madison's proposal shocked Hamilton because the two of them opposed a similar proposal back in 1783. Madison wrote at that time, "To discriminate the merits of these several descriptions of creditors would be a task equally unnecessary & invidious. If the voice of humanity plead more loudly in favour of some than of others; the voice of policy no less than of justice pleads in favour of all."[26] When confronted by Hamilton, Madison admitted that he changed his opinion because of the growth in speculation since 1783.[27]

It is difficult to see how discrimination was "a task equally unnecessary & invidious" in 1783, but was not in 1789, even with the growth of speculation. By the time of this 1789 debate, Jefferson had returned from Paris and had become Madison's political mentor. Much more than Madison, Jefferson was a fanatical opponent of banking and speculation. Upon Jefferson's return to America, Madison followed his lead. As Hamilton wrote, "Mr. Madison had always entertained an exalted opinion of the talents, knowledge, and virtues of Mr. Jefferson. The sentiment was probably reciprocal. A close correspondence subsisted between them during the time of Mr. Jefferson's absence from the country. A close intimacy arose upon his return."[28]

Debt discrimination was one of many times that Madison sided with Jefferson, contradictory to his prior positions. Debt discrimination also demonstrated that the old battle between the angry mobs and Founding Fathers continued. Some of the original holders of the government bonds were the same unpaid soldiers behind Shays' Rebellion, the Newburgh Conspiracy, and the Pennsylvania Mutiny. They wanted the government to do what was "unnecessary & invidious" for their benefit at the expense of those who bought the bonds from them, many of whom bought the bonds not just for speculation but also out of patriotism. Furthermore, many who had sold their government bonds to "stock-jobbers" were themselves "land-jobbers," speculating in land instead of government bonds.[29]

By upholding contract law, redeeming the government's debt at full value, and paying the current holders of the bonds, Alexander Hamilton established solid credit and inviolable property rights, enabling the United States to become a financial superpower.

Hamilton also recommended that the federal government assume all debts owed by the states, most of which were accrued to fund the War for

Independence. Hamilton argued that "the nature of the debt of the United States…was the price of liberty"[30] and that it was the whole nation's responsibility to pay off these debts.

The idea that the federal government should assume the debts of the states was not a new one. Robert Morris proposed it back in 1783.[31] The Constitutional Convention debated this on more than one occasion.[32] At the Convention, John Rutledge of South Carolina argued, "The assumption would be just as the State debts were contracted in the common defence." Charles Pinckney, also from South Carolina, countered that the state debts should "not be viewed in the light of federal expenditures." Roger Sherman of Connecticut thought that "it would be better to authorize the Legislature to assume the State debts, than to say positively it should be done."[33] The Convention left the issue of the assumption of state debts unresolved, leaving it for the new Congress to decide.

As far back as 1781, Hamilton had written to Robert Morris, "A national debt, if it is not excessive, will be to us a national blessing."[34] In 1790, Hamilton explained, "It is a well known fact, that in countries in which the national debt is properly funded, and an object of established confidence, it answers most of the purposes of money. Transfers of stock or public debt are there equivalent to payments in specie."[35] As long as the people trust the government to repay its debt on time, people will use the notes as currency. They will be almost as good as gold. In some ways, they will be even better because notes are easier to carry.

Certain states opposed assumption because they had already paid off most of their debts. Jefferson and the Anti-Federalists opposed it because the federal takeover of this debt would weaken the states further and reward the speculators. Madison, who agreed with Hamilton on this issue in the past, sided with Jefferson and opposed assumption, much to Hamilton's surprise.[36]

Years later, Jefferson would ridicule Hamilton's notion that a federal debt would be a benefit to the nation. In 1813, Jefferson wrote, "At the time we were funding our national debt, we heard much about "a public debt being a public blessing;" that the stock representing it was a creation of active capital for the aliment of commerce, manufactures and agriculture. This paradox was well adapted to the minds of believers in dreams…"[37]

However, Hamilton never favored a permanent debt. In 1795, he proposed "extinguishing the whole of the present debt of the United States, foreign and domestic, in a period not exceeding thirty years."[38] Additionally, Hamilton never favored the creation of more debt. The debt he wanted to assume already existed under the states. Hamilton's goal was to convert it into federal debt and make the interest and principal payments that some of the states had been neglecting.

The House of Representatives voted against assumption, a victory for Jefferson and Madison. At the same time, the government was debating where to locate the new national capital. Jefferson invited Madison and Hamilton for dinner at his New York house to discuss these matters and work out a compromise. Madison and Jefferson agreed to support assumption and the full redemption of debts payable to the current holders in exchange for building the nation's capital on the Potomac River. Jefferson thought he had outsmarted Hamilton. Jefferson thought that locating the capital in the South would influence the government to support the agricultural South over the more industrial North. But as Jefferson later admitted to George Washington, "I was duped into by the Secretary of the Treasury and made a tool for forwarding his schemes, not then sufficiently understood by me; and of all the errors of my political life, this has occasioned me the deepest regret."[39]

Hamilton's assumption of state debt and full redemption without discrimination was an immediate success. European investors recognized that the United States government would fully honor its commitments and would not change the laws to suit political interests. Just as Hamilton predicted, European capital flowed into America and the national debt became "a national blessing."[40]

Alexander Hamilton's most controversial financial proposal was still to come. As far back as 1779, Hamilton argued that the United States needed a private national bank with government backing, similar to the Bank of England and the Bank of Amsterdam, which were the banks behind the world's leading economic powers.[41] In fact, Hamilton was a major proponent of the Bank of North America started by Robert Morris under the Confederation government.

As Secretary of the Treasury, Hamilton proposed the Bank of the United States. With interest and principal to pay off, tax revenue coming in, and government expenditures going out, the federal government needed a bank to help it conduct its business in all thirteen states over an area stretching across more than a thousand miles. Thus, the primary purpose of this national bank was to enable the government to conduct monetary transactions throughout the Union, deposit its cash, and borrow money from other banks.[42]

The national bank would also help regulate the money supply and discipline banks chartered by the states.[43] After the inflation in colonial times and during the War for Independence, the Founding Fathers wrote in the Constitution, "No State shall…make any Thing but gold and silver Coin a Tender in Payment of Debts." James Madison explained, "The power to make any thing but gold and silver a tender in payment of debts, is withdrawn from the States, on the same principle with that of striking of paper currency."[44] However, the Constitution did not prohibit private corporations from issuing bills of credit and the states were already chartering banks that were inflating the money supply.

To restrain the state-chartered banks, the Bank of the United States would set the reserve requirement for banks that wished to do business with it and monitor their reserve levels. Just as the Founding Fathers established the federal government to weaken the state governments, the national bank would weaken the state-chartered banks by regulating their money printing and credit creation.

The government placed strict rules on the Bank of the United States to ensure that it would remain privately owned, free from government manipulation, and not inflate the money supply like the state-chartered banks were doing. The Bank was not allowed to buy government bonds. It could not incur debts or issue notes in excess of its capitalization. The Secretary of the Treasury could inspect the bank's books, but had no say in its operation.

Many Republicans and even some Federalists opposed Hamilton's bank because they opposed banking in general. Thomas Jefferson wrote in 1814, "I have ever been the enemy of banks, not of those discounting for cash, but of those foisting their own paper into circulation, and thus banishing our cash. My zeal against those institutions was so warm and open at the establishment of the Bank of the United States, that I was derided as a maniac by the tribe of bank-mongers, who were seeking to filch from the public their swindling and barren gains."[45]

John Adams also disliked banks. In 1809, Adams wrote, "Our medium is depreciated by the multitude of swindling banks, which have emitted bank bills to an immense amount beyond the deposits of gold and silver in their vaults, by which means the price of labor and land and merchandise and produce is doubled, tripled, and quadrupled in many instances. Every dollar of a bank bill that is issued beyond the quantity of gold and silver in the vaults, represents nothing, and is therefore a cheat upon somebody."[46]

However, most Republicans and state politicians who opposed Hamilton's bank did so because it would take power and money away from the states and state-chartered banks.[47] The majority of Americans had no ideological opposition to banking. Constitutionally speaking, the government had no power to restrict private banking. In fact, the states were already chartering these banks. The only question was whether these banks should be chartered by the states, the federal government, both, or neither.

While just about everybody in the 1790s agreed that the government could not restrict private banking, the Republicans argued that a national bank was unconstitutional. Jefferson and Madison argued that the Constitution did not give the federal government the power to charter a bank. Hamilton countered that the Constitution granted implied powers under the Constitution's "necessary and proper" clause and was quick to point out that Madison agreed with this concept.[48]

The question was not whether the Constitution authorized a national bank, which it clearly did not. Nor was the question whether there were implied powers, which both Hamilton and Madison agreed there were. The question was whether this national bank was "necessary and proper" for the operation of the government.

Jefferson argued that the bank was not "necessary and proper" and therefore unconstitutional. Hamilton replied that "a bank has a natural relation to the power of collecting taxes–to that of borrowing money–to that of regulating trade–to that of providing for the common defence." Hamilton further argued that "banks are essential to the pecuniary operation of the Government."[49]

Hamilton admitted that the bank was not "absolutely necessary," but argued that the Constitution did not include the word "absolutely" and that such a requirement would restrict the government from doing almost anything. Furthermore, if such a standard applied to the state governments it would prohibit them from incorporating banks and even towns, which are not powers expressly given to them by their constitutions.[50]

Therefore, Hamilton argued that the bank need not be "absolutely necessary," but "if the end be clearly comprehended within any of the specified powers, and if the measure have an obvious relation to that end, and is not forbidden by any particular provision of the Constitution, it may safely be deemed to come within the compass of the national authority."[51]

In the end, the Senate easily passed the bank bill, though the vote count and debates were not recorded. In the House, it passed 39 to 19 despite Madison's vehement opposition.[52] President Washington signed the bill. The Supreme Court unanimously upheld it in 1819.[53] Thomas Jefferson kept the bank throughout his administration. James Madison supported renewing the charter of the Bank of the United States in 1811, but the bill failed by a single vote in both the House and the Senate. In 1816, Madison signed the bill chartering the Second Bank of the United States. So despite the vocal opposition, most people, even most Republicans, saw the necessity and constitutionality of Hamilton's Bank of the United States.

PROSPERITY AND TRANQUILITY

Alexander Hamilton's financial system was an immediate success. Inflation disappeared, the government paid the interest on its debt, the banking system grew but remained stable, the United States received a solid credit rating, and the economy expanded.

From the government's perspective, Hamilton's Bank of the United States was a very profitable venture. The federal government invested $2 million in 1791 and sold the last of its shares in 1802. In that time, it earned dividends of more than $1.1 million and capital gains of nearly $700,000—a return in excess of eight percent a year.[54]

Even with the Bank of the United States, state-chartered banks continued supplying most of the currency in circulation.[55] The job of the Bank of the United States was to act as an indirect regulator of these state-chartered banks, which it did successfully. Because the Bank of the United States was the nation's largest bank and had the backing of the federal government, other banks trusted it and wanted to do business with it. The Bank of the United States ensured that its banking partners held sufficient reserves, even when the states that chartered them had no reserve requirements.[56] As a result, no bank "became insolvent or even failed to redeem its notes in specie on demand" during the Federalist era.[57]

The success of the Bank of the United States sparked rapid growth in the banking sector. The United States had just three state-chartered banks in 1790, but that rose to twenty-nine by 1800 and eighty-nine by 1811.[58] Between 1790 and 1811, when the charter of the Bank of the United States expired, the capital stock of state-chartered banks rose from $3 million to $52 million.[59] And thanks to the Bank of the United States, the new nation had one of the most reliable money supplies in the world.[60]

During the Federalist era, most of the government's meager budget went to pay interest on the debt.[61] If the Federalists wanted to pay down the debt, they would have had to raise taxes. Washington and Hamilton chose low taxes and a fairly steady debt level rather than raise taxes. Hamilton also preferred a manageable national debt to higher taxes because people could use the government notes as currency, increasing the velocity of money in the economy.[62] Furthermore, as the American population and economy grew, the relatively stable debt level became less burdensome. Although federal government debt rose 9.9 percent in the 1790s, debt per person fell from $18.54 in 1791 to $15.62 in 1800, a 15.7 percent decrease.[63] Relative to the overall economy, debt fell from 35 percent of gross domestic product in 1792 to 17 percent by 1800, a greater than 50 percent reduction.[64]

By reliably paying interest on the debt, the credit of the United States immediately went from one of the worst in the world to one of the best. George Washington wrote in 1791, "Our public credit stands on that ground, which three years ago it would have been a species of madness to have foretold. The astonishing rapidity, with which the newly instituted Bank was filled, gives an unexampled proof of the resources of our Countrymen, and their confidence in public measures."[65]

The United States went from having a worthless Dollar and no credit under the Articles of Confederation to the best credit rating in the world within a few years. In fact, by 1794, United States bonds sold for a ten percent premium over face value, whereas before they had traded at a huge discount.[66]

With solid credit established, thanks to Hamilton's financial system, foreign trade increased and the economy expanded. Along with the government's improved credit, private credit became more accessible. As Hamilton pointed out, "Public and private credit are closely allied, if not inseparable."[67]

Foreign trade increased rapidly in the 1790s as the United States de-clared neutrality and traded with both France and Britain. Jeremy Atack and Peter Passell write in *A New Economic View of American History: From Colonial Times to 1940*, "Exports doubled between 1792 and 1795. Then doubled again by 1801 and, by 1807, were five times what they had been just fifteen years earlier." In contrast, exports rose only thirty percent between 1770 and 1790.[68]

With a steady stream of government revenue, strong credit, capital inflows from Europe, and a stable money supply, the United States economy recovered quickly from the turmoil of the War for Independ-ence and the struggles under the Confederation. The effects were immediate. After just two years as President, George Washington explained, "The United States enjoy a scene of prosperity and tranquillity under the new government, that could hardly have been hoped for under the old." The following day, Washington added, "Tranquillity reigns among the people, with that disposition towards the general government, which is likely to preserve it. They begin to feel the good effects of equal laws and equal protection."[69]

The expanding economy and sharp rise in exports boosted American shipping. American ships operated at half the expense of British ships because of the country's plentiful lumber and because America built smaller but faster ships. Additionally, the United States instituted tariffs designed to benefit American shipping. As a result, the United States' market share of British-American trade went from 50 percent in 1790 to 95 percent in 1800. To carry all these goods across the ocean, the total tonnage of American ships tripled in 1790 alone and kept growing for many years to come. Though the United States ran a trade deficit, the shipping industry made such a large profit that the new nation ran a net surplus in world trade. As a result, the supply of gold and silver increased and America's money shortage disappeared.[70]

The increase in trade, capturing of market share, and productivity gains led to a quadrupling of wages for American sailors. Likewise, the average wage for an American laborer nearly quadrupled between 1790 and 1811, increasing at an average annual rate of over six percent.[71]

In the 1790s and early 1800s, the American economy expanded, businesses profited, and the wages of American laborers rose. The rising tide from Hamilton's financial system lifted all boats.

ANGRY MOBS IN THE REPUBLIC

The United States under George Washington's presidency was a tremendous success, but it was not without troubles. On a couple of issues, angry mobs opposed the new federal government and threatened to plunge the nation back into chaos and anarchy.

The tariffs of 1789 were just enough to fund the government and pay interest on the federal debt. When the federal government assumed the state debts, it needed an additional $825,000 a year to pay the interest.[72] Hamilton proposed an excise tax on spirits. Farmers in the west objected. Because of the difficulty and cost of shipping their grain to the urban centers along the Atlantic seaboard, western farmers turned their grain into whiskey, which was easier and cheaper to transport. The burden of this tax on spirits would fall disproportionately on them.

Refusing to pay the tax on whiskey, thousands of poor western farmers rebelled against the government. Angry about the new tax and their economic plight in general, these protestors, joined by others who did not even produce whiskey, attacked tax collectors and also wealthy people who had nothing to do with the whiskey tax. The political protest had turned into an unruly mob, attacking anybody who did not join their cause.

President George Washington gathered an army of nearly 13,000 troops, a force larger than he had commanded during most of the War for Independence. As Washington led the army toward battle, the rebels fled and the insurrection fell apart. In a speech to Congress, Washington condemned these "enemies of order" who "labored for an ascendency over the will of others by the guidance of their passions, produced symptoms of riot and violence."[73] In a letter to Secretary of State Edmund Randolph, Washington wrote, "My mind is so perfectly convinced, that, if these self-created societies cannot be discountenanced, they will destroy the government of this country."[74]

While the Whiskey Rebellion was a direct attack on the government and involved thousands of rebels, it was confined to just five counties in western Pennsylvania and was unlikely to spread. In contrast, the issue of whether to ally with Britain or France whipped the entire country into a frenzy. The events of the French Revolution forced Americans to re-evaluate the meaning of their revolution while a French foreign minister tested the balance of power between the people and the government.

Many Americans saw the French Revolution as a continuation and copy of the American Revolution. They saw the French Revolution as a democratic revolution against monarchy, just like the American Revolution had been. Many even thought that the success of the United States depended on the outcome of the French Revolution. Thomas Jefferson wrote in 1791 that the French Revolution was "necessary to stay up our own and to prevent it from falling back to that kind of half-way-house, the English constitution."[75]

Though America won its independence long ago and the United States had its Constitution, Jefferson continued to fight for the ideals of the American Revolution—the spirit of '76. Thomas Jefferson, and Thomas Paine too, were not just revolutionaries. They were romantics. Their infatuation with revolution and democracy led them to support destructive democratic uprisings. They saw the success of the American Revolution in other revolutions, even if those others only created chaos, death, and destruction. As Jefferson wrote in 1793, "The liberty of the whole earth was depending on the issue of the contest, and was ever such a prize won with so little innocent blood? My own affections have been deeply wounded by some of the martyrs to this cause, but rather than it should have failed I would have seen half the earth desolated; were there but an Adam and an Eve left in every country, and left free, it would be better than as it now is."[76]

Another group, those who preferred law, order, and stability, viewed the French Revolution as lawless and chaotic. They argued that the French Revolution bore little similarity to the American Revolution. Alexander Hamilton wrote in 1793, "There is no real resemblance between what was the cause of America and what is the cause of France; that the difference is no less great than that between liberty and licentiousness." Additionally, a number of Founding Fathers, including George Washington and Gouverneur Morris, as well as Edmund Burke in Britain, predicted the French Revolution would end with a military dictator.[77]

When France went to war with Britain, the American people were sharply divided about which nation to support. America was so split that President Washington ran for reelection in 1792 only because he worried the North and the South would fight a civil war without his unifying influence. Being about more than just slavery, this civil war would have been about which side to support in the Franco-British conflict and the extent of the powers of the federal government, especially as it related to Hamilton's bank.[78]

Recognizing America's divided opinion about the Franco-British war and the French Revolution, Edmond-Charles Genet came to America to convince the United States to support France. Genet toured the country and met with the people, primarily in the South where pro-French sentiment was stronger. While Genet's official job was to negotiate with the United States government, he and others in France recognized that a large percentage of the people were strong supporters of the French Revolution while most of those in government, including Washington and Hamilton, opposed the disorder, lawlessness, and bloodshed occurring in France.

Furthermore, Genet's official title was "Minister Plenipotentiary of the French Republic to the Congress of the United States."[79] Even though the Constitution states that the President "shall have Power, by and with the

Advice and Consent of the Senate, to make Treaties," the French believed that only Congress represented the people, just as France's National Convention was the sole representative of the French people, holding both legislative and executive powers. Therefore, Genet spoke to the people and worked with Congress while largely ignoring President Washington.[80]

Genet seduced many Americans to the French cause, but he did not sway the Federalists, who controlled the reins of government. President Washington issued the Proclamation of Neutrality, declaring the United States to be "impartial" in the conflict between Britain and France. While Jefferson and the Republicans hoped Washington would side with the French, Hamilton and the Federalists hoped Washington would use the word "neutral," a stronger term than "impartial." Washington compromised, in part because the Republicans argued that the President had no power to declare neutrality.[81] Jefferson even convinced Madison that the Proclamation of Neutrality was unconstitutional, though they changed their positions later when it became obvious that France was falling apart and the Federalists were right to maintain neutrality.[82]

Shortly thereafter, the United States and Britain signed the Jay Treaty resolving some longstanding disputes and enabling the two countries to avert war and trade freely with each other. The Republicans opposed this treaty, still favoring France in the European war. However, even with this treaty, the United States remained impartial and was free to trade with both European nations. James Madison tried to block the Jay Treaty in the House of Representatives by demanding Washington turn over any papers related to it. Washington refused because the House had no say in treaties. The Jay Treaty was approved and the United States stayed impartial and traded with all willing partners. America enjoyed peace and prosperity while Europe was mired in chaos.

THE FALL OF THE FEDERALISTS

Throughout the 1790s, the Federalists had near total control of the government. Thomas Jefferson resigned from his post as Secretary of State at the end of 1793, after the Genet affair and the Proclamation of Neutrality but before the Jay Treaty. As a member of Washington's cabinet, Jefferson was limited in how he could oppose the administration he worked for. By detaching himself from George Washington and the Federalist government, Jefferson could more actively oppose the Federalists. Nevertheless, in 1796, John Adams narrowly beat out Jefferson for the Presidency.

Angry that the United States declared neutrality and signed the Jay Treaty with Britain, the French navy captured American ships trading with Britain. President John Adams sent Charles Cotesworth Pinckney to negotiate with the French, but France demanded a bribe to meet with him. In response, the United States revoked all treaties with France, built up its navy, and authorized attacks on French warships. The Quasi-War with France had begun.

Despite the bloodshed of the French Revolution, Republicans continued to favor France over Britain and opposed this war. To silence his critics, President John Adams signed the Alien and Sedition Acts into law. The Alien Act enabled the President to deport aliens "dangerous to the peace and safety of the United States." The Sedition Act made it unlawful "to combine or conspire together to oppose any measure of the government of the United States" or "to write, print, utter or publish, or cause it to be done, or assist in it, any false, scandalous, and malicious writing against the government of the United States, or either House of Congress, or the President, with intent to defame, or bring either into contempt or disrepute, or to excite against either the hatred of the people of the United States, or to stir up sedition, or to excite unlawful combinations against the government, or to resist it, or to aid or encourage hostile designs of foreign nations."

Republicans vehemently opposed these unconstitutional acts. James Madison penned the Virginia Resolutions while Thomas Jefferson wrote the Kentucky Resolutions, arguing that the states had the right to nullify unconstitutional laws and interpose between the federal government and the people.[83] More important, Jefferson and the Republicans made the Alien and Sedition Acts the primary issue of the 1800 election. The Federalists were divided as Hamilton, now working in the private sector, recommended Charles Cotesworth Pinckney instead of President John Adams as the Federalist nominee for President.

The Republicans swept into office. Jefferson won the Presidency. The Republicans captured both houses of Congress as the Federalists lost 7 of their 22 Senate seats and 22 of their 60 House seats. The Federalist Party would never again return to power.

THE FEDERALIST REPUBLICANS

The Presidential election of 1800 resulted in a tie between Thomas Jefferson and Aaron Burr, both Republicans. This sent the election to the House of Representatives, where Jefferson won eight states, Burr won six, and two states were tied and cast blank ballots. Many Northern Federalists voted for the more moderate Burr, who hailed from New York, rather than vote for the Jefferson, the Southern radical Republican. To win a majority of the states, Jefferson needed some of these Federalist representatives to switch their votes or at least withdraw their votes for Burr.

Although most Federalists preferred Burr to Jefferson, Alexander Hamilton endorsed his long-time rival Jefferson for President. Hamilton argued that Jefferson was preferable to Burr because, "As to Burr, there is nothing in his favour. His private character is not defended by his most partial friends. He is bankrupt beyond redemption except by the plunder of his country. His public principles have no other spring or aim than his own aggrandisement… If he can, he will certainly disturb our institutions to secure to himself permanent power and with it wealth. He is truly the Cataline of America."[84]

Even with Hamilton's endorsement, no Federalists switched their votes to Jefferson as the House of Representatives cast thirty-five ballots with no winner. Hamilton was no longer in government and had lost much of his influence after the disclosure of his affair with Maria Reynolds in 1797 and after Washington's death in 1799. Finally, after the Federalists received assurances from Jefferson's supporters that Jefferson would keep Hamilton's financial system, would not fire Federalists working for the government, would maintain neutrality, and would not shrink the navy, some Federalists cast blank ballots in the thirty-sixth round of voting, swinging two more states into Jefferson's column and giving him the victory.

Honor bound by the agreement made by his supporters, but also seeing the success of Hamilton's financial system, Jefferson made few changes to it. In his First Inaugural Address, Jefferson stated, "Would the honest patriot, in the full tide of successful experiment, abandon a government which has so far kept us free and firm, on the theoretic and visionary fear that this government, the world's best hope, may by possibility want energy to preserve itself? I trust not. I believe this, on the contrary, the strongest government on earth. I believe it the only one where every man, at the call of the laws, would fly to the standard of the law, and would meet invasions of the public order as his own personal concern." Trying to unite the country, Jefferson also remarked, "We have called by different names brethren of the same principle. We are all republicans–we are all federalists."[85]

Even though the Republicans won the political battle against the Federalists, the institutions and programs set up by the Federalists continued under the Republicans. Jefferson and the Republicans took the best of what the Federalists had created and made it their own, including Hamilton's financial system. Although America embraced the ideology of Jeffersonian democracy, the Federalist system continued for decades. As a result, the American economy continued to expand.

Despite the promise of his supporters, Jefferson looked for ways to close down the Bank of the United States. If he could find fraud or other illegal activity, he would have the excuse he needed to revoke the charter of the national bank. Upon taking office, Jefferson had Treasury Secretary Albert Gallatin inspect the Treasury Department's actions under Hamilton. After conducting a thorough investigation, Gallatin told Jefferson, "I have found the most perfect system ever formed—any change that should be made in it would injure it—Hamilton made no blunders—committed no frauds. He did nothing wrong."[86]

Jefferson conceded this in a letter to Dupont de Nemours, "We can pay off his debt in 15 years: but we can never get rid of his financial system. It mortifies me to be strengthening principles which I deem radically vicious, but this vice is entailed on us by the first error."[87] Consequently, Jefferson oversaw a huge expansion of banking. When he came into office, there were just twenty-nine banks in the United States.

By 1811, there were eighty-nine.[88] Many of the "Old Republicans" believed Jefferson had abandoned his principles when he refused to dismantle Hamilton's financial system.[89]

Jefferson also made relatively few changes to the government's spending and taxes. Government revenue rose from nothing to more than $10 million under the Federalists and rose to $17 million by the end of Jefferson's second term, more a function of the growing economy than any drastic changes in tax policy. The one major change made by the Republicans was the elimination of internal taxes, including the excise tax on whiskey and other spirits, which had brought in up to $1.5 million in revenue per year. Meanwhile, the Republicans kept government spending in check. This produced a budget surplus and the Republicans retired nearly half of the national debt by 1813.[90]

When the Bank of the United States came up for renewal in 1811, President James Madison and Treasury Secretary Albert Gallatin both supported renewing the bank, but most Republicans wanted to destroy it. Renewal of the bank failed by a single vote in both the House and the Senate, with Madison's own Vice President—the Anti-Federalist George Clinton—breaking a tie in the Senate by voting against the bill Madison supported.

Without the restraint that the Bank of the United States exerted over the state-chartered banks, bank balance sheets boomed. The number of banks rose from 89 in 1811 to 208 in 1815. From 1811 to 1814, the value of notes in circulation doubled whereas specie rose by sixty-seven percent. Inflation picked up and banks stopped redeeming their notes.[91]

At the same time, the United States government increased spending to fight the War of 1812 against Britain while tariff revenue declined as the Napoleonic Wars in Europe curtailed foreign trade. Madison and the Republicans reinstituted internal taxes but the national debt still rose dramatically.[92] The Republicans had no choice but to charter the Second Bank of the United States to help fund the war and to restrain the state-chartered banks, just as the first bank had done.[93]

In total, the finances of the federal government under Washington, Adams, and Jefferson differed little. Government spending stayed around two percent of gross domestic product and non-interest spending was around one percent during the administrations of the first three Presidents. However, spending rose sharply under Madison because of the War of 1812.[94]

Federal Government Spending as a Percentage of GDP[95]

	Expenditures	Interest Expense	Non-Interest Expenditures
Washington	2.0%	1.1%	0.9%
Adams	2.0%	0.7%	1.3%
Jefferson	1.7%	0.7%	1.0%
Madison	2.6%	0.5%	2.1%

In 1816, the Republicans chartered the Second Bank of the United States. The Second Bank ushered in another era of financial and economic stability. The number of banks increased more slowly during the period of the Second Bank of the United States than before or after it.[96] In total, the Republicans maintained the Federalist financial system, including the national bank, for most of their twenty-four years in power.

In 1832, President Andrew Jackson ran for reelection promising to eliminate the Second Bank of the United States. Although the Second Bank of the United States was not as successful as the first, the destruction of the Second Bank caused America's deepest depression up to that time.

The charter of the Second Bank of the United States was not set to expire until 1836. President Jackson did not want to wait that long, so he withdrew the government's deposits beginning in 1833 and distributed it to twenty-three different state-chartered banks, many of whose officers supported Jackson in the 1832 election.[97]

Andrew Jackson's own Vice President, Martin Van Buren, warned Jackson not to withdraw the government's money from the Second Bank. Nicholas Biddle, President of the Second Bank of the United States, predicted that withdrawing deposits from the Bank and letting its charter expire would lead to a speculative bubble.[98] By removing the restraint provided by the Second Bank of the United States, Andrew Jackson created a bubble while, at the same time, reduced confidence in the American banking sector.[99]

Between 1829 and 1837, Jackson's first and last years in office, the number of banks rose from 329 to 788, the amount of banknotes tripled, and the value of loans outstanding quadrupled.[100] In 1835 alone, the number of banks jumped 39 percent from 506 to 704. In the following two years, the money supply increased by about 60 percent and commodity prices rose more than 30 percent. People used this easy credit to speculate on land in the West, which could be bought cheaply from the federal government. The government then distributed the surplus revenue from its land sales back to the people, which they used to buy even more land, creating a vicious cycle of credit and speculation.[101]

By 1836, Andrew Jackson recognized that the loose lending standards of the state-chartered banks created a bubble. He issued an executive order, the Specie Circular, requiring all government land sales be paid for in gold or silver, not bank notes. The Specie Circular burst the bubble and also exposed overinvestment in capital projects, especially canals.

The Panic of 1837 lasted only a year but a second panic followed in 1839. From its peak in 1836 to its trough in 1842, money supply decreased by more than 40 percent and prices also fell by about 40 percent. Ninety percent of factories closed. Full recovery would take a decade.[102]

The federal government suffered big losses in this depression. Federal revenue fell in half, declining to its lowest level in decades.[103] The federal government lost $9 million in deposits when many of the banks it used and hundreds of others failed.[104] However, the federal government's loss was nothing compared with that of the states.

In the 1820s and 1830s, the states spent and borrowed millions of dollars building canals, expecting no profits for many years to come, if ever. The general decline in prices increased the burden of the debt that the states had incurred. At the same time, the economic slowdown reduced the expected revenues of the canals. With tax revenue declining, heavy debt burdens, and insufficient credit, many states failed to make their debt payments. Eight states defaulted on their debts, as did the territory of Florida. Four of them repudiated their debts and never paid them back.[105]

Individuals also had a debt problem because they had borrowed to join in on the speculative land rush that was supported by the loose credit. Congress passed a new bankruptcy law forgiving $441 million in debt owed by 39,000 people because there was not enough space for all those people in debtors' prisons.[106] That loss to creditors represented nearly thirty percent of gross domestic product.[107]

Little evidence exists to suggest that the First or Second Banks of the United States damaged the nation's finances or economy. To the contrary, the evidence indicates that the national banks helped the country fund its debts, restrained state-chartered banks, and prevented unwarranted credit expansion.

The evidence also suggests that free banking resulted in bubbles and depressions during the Confederation, between 1811 and 1816, and after the Second Bank's expiration in the 1830s. There were more bank failures and panics under free banking than under the First and Second Banks of the United States. Furthermore, after the depression of the late 1830s and early 1840s, gold and silver coins largely replaced gold and silver notes. This raised the total interest cost in the economy.[108]

Besides keeping the financial system that they had so vigorously opposed in the 1790s, the Republicans acted like Federalists in other ways. In the 1790s, the Republicans complained about Federalist protectionism. But in 1807, Jefferson cut off all foreign trade with the Embargo Act and the United States navy blockaded American ports. Exports fell eighty percent—back to where they were in 1792—and tariff revenue declined with it.[109] New England used Jefferson's idea of nullification to declare the 1807 trade embargo unconstitutional and ignored it by smuggling goods in and out of America, just as they had done to avoid British mercantilism and taxes in colonial times. The War of 1812 destroyed what little remained of international trade as Britain blockaded American ports. Exports fell to nearly nothing and foreign trade would not permanently recover to the level of the early 1800s until the late 1840s.[110]

One side effect of Jefferson's embargo was the accelerated development of American industry. Whereas only 4 new factories were incorporated in 1807, 26 new factories were incorporated in 1809. The War of 1812 led to even more factory building, with 128 new factories incorporated in 1814. In *A New Economic View of American History: From Colonial Times to 1940*, Jeremy Atack and Peter Passell reckon that "the embargo thus achieved what Alexander Hamilton had desired and

Jefferson had feared: the beginnings of industrialization."[111] Curtis Nettels writes in *The Emergence of a National Economy: 1775-1815*, "The embargo and the War of 1812 did more than Hamilton's *Report on Manufactures* to popularize factories and machines."[112] However, by the 1810s, the Jeffersonians realized the value of manufacturing.[113] In 1816, Jefferson explained, "Within the thirty years which have elapsed, how are circumstances changed! … Experience has taught me that manufactures are now as necessary to our independence as to our comfort."[114]

When trade resumed after the war, only eight new factories were incorporated in 1817. Many of those built during the war years went bankrupt.[115] In effect, the trade restrictions of Jefferson's embargo and the War of 1812 encouraged investment in unprofitable industrial ventures. Though America was already moving toward industrialization, it would not fully embrace it until the 1840s. As a result, America had wasted precious capital because of the Embargo Act of 1807 and the War of 1812.

In the 1790s, Republicans opposed Federalist attempts to increase the federal debt when Hamilton proposed assuming state debts. However, the Republicans had no qualms about purchasing Louisiana from France in 1803 and borrowing $15 million to do so, an option only made possible by Hamilton's financial system and the solid credit rating he established.

The Louisiana Purchase faced opposition. Some Americans were concerned about granting citizenship to the French and Spanish living in the territory because they were unfamiliar with America's political systems. Others worried that Napoleon would renege on the sale of Louisiana and that America lacked the military strength to keep the territory. Others pointed out that the United States was purchasing a territory and would administer it without the consent of its citizens, against the principles of the Declaration of Independence and the American Revolution. Furthermore, the residents of Louisiana would have no vote, no representation, and no trial by jury, but would be taxed.[116]

More important, the Constitution did not grant the United States government the power to purchase territories. Jefferson even admitted that the "constitution has made no provision for our holding foreign territory, still less for incorporating foreign nations into our Union." He admits that he went "beyond the Constitution" for "the good of their country" and that the "Legislature…must ratify and pay for it, and throw themselves on their country for doing for them unauthorized, what we know they would have done for themselves had they been in a situation to do it."[117] Despite the valid arguments against the Louisiana purchase, Jefferson betrayed some of his principles to take advantage of this unique opportunity.

When the Federalists controlled the government in the 1790s, the Republicans argued against debt, against the national bank, against protectionism, and for a strict construction of the Constitution. However, when faced with the realities of governing, Thomas Jefferson and the Republicans adopted the Federalist policies and institutions that successfully guided the infant United States through the 1790s. As a result, Jefferson and the Republicans created a synthesis between the philosophy of Jeffersonian democracy and the institutions and governance of the Federalists.

WESTWARD EXPANSION

Westward expansion was one of the driving forces behind the American Revolution. After the French and Indian War, the British tried to prevent Americans from settling the West. Especially in the South, American loyalty to Britain declined as the royal government failed to defend the settlers against Indian attacks. With the founding of the United States, westward expansion continued to be a major issue for another century. It would provide the United States with many benefits, but also create a number of problems for the young nation.

In the early years of the United States, the case for westward expansion was weak. Excluding the areas along rivers, transportation of produce from the West to the East was slow and expensive. Local communities still developed, but without the means of affordable transportation, western settlements relied primarily on subsistence farming.

For the first few years, frontier agriculture did not even provide a farmer and his family what they needed for themselves. It took about a month to clear just one acre of land, but a family farm usually required about fifty acres. Over the course of about five years, a farmer could clear enough land to establish a profitable farm.[118] As a result, frontier farming consumed years worth of savings, wasting precious capital in a nation that had little to begin with.[119]

In *A New Economic View of American History: From Colonial Times to 1940*, Jeremy Atack and Peter Passell argue that standards of living grew slowly or may have even have fallen between 1775 and 1820 because "rapid geographic expansion represented a serious drag on agricultural labor productivity, depressing per capita income levels in the dominant sector of the economy." They add that the transition from agriculture to industry, with its higher rate of productivity, "might have occurred sooner and with less political and social disruption had it not been for the federal policy of selling land cheaply or giving it away."[120]

Alexander Hamilton predicted this in his 1790 *Report on a National Bank*:

> The progressive settlement of the former, while it promises ample retribution, in the generation of future resources, diminishes or obstructs, in the mean time, the active wealth of the country. It not only draws off a part of the circulating money, and places it in a more passive state, but it diverts, into its own channels, a portion of that species of labor and industry which would otherwise be employed in furnishing materials for foreign trade, and which, by contributing to a favorable balance, would assist the introduction of specie. In the early periods of new settlements, the settlers not only furnish no surplus for exportation, but they consume a part of that which is produced by the labor of others.[121]

The expansion into the west, a key argument for revolution among many Americans, might have done more harm than good to the nation's developing economy. America was starving for capital and, instead of investing it propitiously, it spent dearly to improve new land that was not yet profitable. Westward expansion also slowed America's urbanization and industrialization. As a result, the average standard of living for Americans did not improve significantly until the 1840s.[122]

The West was settled hastily, in part, because Jefferson and the Republicans favored selling the land in small parcels for low prices. In contrast, Hamilton and the Federalists believed this land should be sold as dearly as possible and be a source of revenue for the government. Thus, upon gaining power, Jefferson subsidized westward expansion and agricultural production through land sales at below-market prices, which only fueled speculation, a vice that Jefferson loathed so much. In addition to selling the land cheaply, the government subsidized roads, river improvements, canals, and railroads. If the settlers had to pay the full cost of the land and transportation, westward expansion would have progressed much more slowly.

Vast improvements in transportation finally made the development of the West worthwhile, but not before squandering more capital. Private businesses started building roads through the Appalachian Mountains with the federal government providing funds for their construction. While these roads made travel and shipping of goods more reliable and less costly, horse-drawn carriages were still slow and inefficient methods of transport. Whereas the productivity of roads doubled between 1815 and 1860, the productivity of ocean transport increased fivefold during that time while that of shipping on western rivers increased at least tenfold.[123]

Improved river travel provided the first significant productivity gains in transportation enabling profitable western settlement. Between 1819 and 1830, steamboat productivity more than quadrupled, though gains thereafter were smaller. Flatboats continued to compete with steamboats in downstream shipping, but steamboats provided a significant advantage in upstream shipping compared to flatboats, which could not go upstream, and keelboats, which were slow because they required laborers to push or pull the boat by pole, from land, or using overhead branches. Thanks to the steamboat, upstream freight rates fell by about ninety percent between 1816 and the 1830s and then fell another fifty percent by the 1850s.[124]

However, steamboats and river improvements only promoted transportation and reduced shipping rates in the narrow areas near navigable rivers. Most rivers were too small for steamboats and even the navigable ones were less efficient than sailing on open water. Even though steam-boats were faster, sailboats were cheaper to build and their means of propulsion wasted less space by not needing an engine or fuel to be carried on board. By 1850, over forty years after Robert Fulton first steamed up and down the Hudson River, steamboats carried just a third of the cargo on the Great Lakes, ten percent along the coast, and just four percent of international trade.[125]

Even though steamboats and river improvements proved valuable, their total contribution was quite limited. Furthermore, most of the western rivers fell under federal control and the federal government paid for many of the river improvements, such as widening and deepening rivers or clearing them of debris. Again, the government was subsidizing westward expansion and distorting its economic costs and benefits.

The construction of canals proved an even bigger boost to westward expansion, but was an even bigger waste of resources. In 1816, there were just one hundred miles of canals in the United States. The longest canal was just twenty-seven miles long and only three exceeded two miles in length.[126] Though the Erie Canal was completed in 1825, most canals were not built until the late 1830s and early 1840s. Canal construction peaked in 1839 and 1840, right in the middle of the country's worst depression.

Except in a few rare cases, such as the Erie Canal, canals yielded low or negative returns. The private sector recognized this and invested little in canals. Instead, state governments provided seventy-three percent of the funding. The states borrowed much of this money and a few de-faulted on these debts.[127] Like with roads and river improvements, the federal government also subsidized canal construction through land grants to the states. So while canals certainly reduced the cost and time to transport goods,[128] it was done at the expense of the taxpayers and bondholders.

After 1840, canal construction dropped sharply as shipping rates and canal profitability declined because of increased competition from the more versatile and profitable railroads. By 1860, America had 30,000 miles of track and had invested five times as much money in rail as in canals.[129] Again, the government subsidized this expansion of transportation, though they had learned a few lessons from the canal bubble and crash. The federal and state governments provided land grants for railroads, though they received free troop transportation and low rates for mail transport in exchange. Whereas the federal government provided funds for canal building, road construction, and river improvements, it did not outlay money for the railroads. It only provided the land and, in fact, kept about half the surrounding land for itself. As a result, governments took little risk and made a hefty profit in many cases as land values rose along railroad routes. Furthermore, while the government gave away land worth about $400 million, the railroads invested about $8 billion in track and equipment between the years of 1850 and 1880.[130]

Railroad construction had a much larger effect on westward expansion than roads, river improvements, and canals, which is what enabled private businesses to earn a profit building and running railroads. Canals and improved roads cut in half the travel time into the interior, but railroads cut it by an additional eighty to ninety percent. In 1800, it took two weeks to travel from New York City to Ohio. Canals and improved roads reduced that to a week. Railroads then reduced that to a day. Traveling from New York City to Chicago took six weeks in 1800, three weeks in 1830, and just two days by 1857.[131] The railroads fundamentally transformed the American interior and finally made westward expansion a profitable and productive venture, though this was many decades after the American colonists protested against a British line of demarcation closing off the West to white settlers.

Additionally, the deployment of the telegraph across America in the 1840s and 1850s helped farmers and manufacturers produce goods in the correct quantities and transport them to the locations where demand and prices were highest. With the railroad and the telegraph, the West grew quickly and profitably.

The settlement of the west, especially after the railroads were built, also helped the Eastern economy by facilitating further specialization. For example, the Northeast became more industrialized when it started importing its produce instead of growing it locally. In 1820, 58 percent of Massachusetts laborers worked in agriculture. By 1840, it had fallen to 40 percent. By 1850, just 15 percent worked in agriculture.[132]

Though the United States had some vigorous debates in its initial years and wasted valuable resources on popular experiments, the new nation had more successes than failures. The Constitution had given the federal government the power to restrain the states, defend property rights, establish a stable financial system, and put down rebellions. Although the Federalists and Republicans argued about political philosophy—or maybe because they argued—the United States found "the perfect balance between liberty and power,"[133] a balance that ensured "prosperity and tranquillity under the new government."[134]

EPILOGUE

In colonial America, thousands of Patriots believed that violent protests would win them independence and freedom. Others believed that uncontrolled rebellion would lead to anarchy and tyranny and instead supported a more cautious course of action. The question for America was whether it should start a revolution with its violence, chaos, and rapid change or if it should evolve gradually in a more peaceful and orderly fashion but that many would see as too slow.

Many political philosophers argue that each society and each generation should live under the form of government it chooses. In *Rights of Man*, Thomas Paine argues, "Every age and generation must be as free to act for itself in all cases as the age and generations which preceded it."[1]

Thomas Jefferson's Declaration of Independence expresses a similar sentiment: "That whenever any Form of Government becomes destructive of these ends, it is the Right of the People to alter or to abolish it, and to institute new Government." The Declaration of Independence also argues, "When a long train of abuses and usurpations, pursuing invariably the same Object evinces a design to reduce them under absolute Despotism, it is their right, it is their duty, to throw off such Government, and to provide new Guards for their future security."

Unlike Paine, who argues that a government may be overthrown "in all cases," the Declaration of Independence implies that it should only be done when the government is "destructive" or at a point of "absolute Despotism." Likewise, the Declaration of Independence declares, "Governments long established should not be changed for light and transient causes."

As the Federalists fought the Republicans and the Constitution challenged the Declaration of Independence for primacy among America's

founding documents, Thomas Jefferson became a more ardent revolutionary, more along the lines of Thomas Paine. In November 1787, as the
Constitution awaited ratification by the states, Jefferson wrote, "God
forbid we should ever be twenty years without such a rebellion... The
tree of liberty must be refreshed from time to time with the blood of
patriots and tyrants. It is it's natural manure."[2] The Constitution had not
even been approved and its provisions had not yet been tested, but
Jefferson was already looking forward to future revolutions.

Speaking about the French Revolution in 1793, Jefferson wrote, "The
liberty of the whole earth was depending on the issue of the contest, and
was ever such a prize won with so little innocent blood? My own affections have been deeply wounded by some of the martyrs to this cause,
but rather than it should have failed I would have seen half the earth
desolated; were there but an Adam and an Eve left in every country, and
left free, it would be better than as it now is."[3] Those are the kinds of
words one would expect to hear from the most extreme revolutionary,
not from the nation's Secretary of State.

In contrast to his Declaration of Independence, which argues that
people have the right and duty to rebel when government is destructive
and despotic, Jefferson abandoned those restrictions by 1816. Jefferson
argued:

> Some men look at constitutions with sanctimonious rever-
> ence, and deem them like the ark of the covenant, too sa-
> cred to be touched. They ascribe to the men of the
> preceding age a wisdom more than human, and suppose
> what they did to be beyond amendment... Each generation
> is as independent of the one preceding, as that was of all
> which had gone before. It has then, like them, a right to
> choose for itself the form of government it believes most
> promotive of its own happiness... It is now forty years since
> the constitution of Virginia was formed. The same tables
> inform us, that, within that period, two-thirds of the adults
> then living are now dead. Have then the remaining third,
> even if they had the wish, the right to hold in obedience to

their will, and to laws heretofore made by them, the other two-thirds, who, with themselves, compose the present mass of adults? ... That majority, then, has a right to depute representatives to a convention, and to make the constitution what they think will be the best for themselves.[4]

Another school of thought argues that each generation inherits its government and could only change its constitution through established and legal means. Edmund Burke argues, "Society is indeed a contract... a partnership not only between those who are living, but between those who are living, those who are dead, and those who are to be born."[5] This is in direct contradiction to Thomas Jefferson, who wrote in 1813, "The earth belongs to the living, not the dead... We may consider each generation as a distinct nation, with a right, by the will of its majority, to bind themselves, but none to bind the succeeding generation, more than the inhabitants of another country."[6]

The Founding Fathers who wrote the Constitution agreed with Burke, not with Jefferson. In a letter to Alexander Hamilton, James Madison explained, "The Constitution requires an adoption in toto, and for ever... An adoption for a limited time would be as defective as an adoption of some of the articles only."[7]

In his farewell address, George Washington explained the fixed nature of the Constitution:

> If, in the opinion of the people, the distribution or modification of the constitutional powers be in any particular wrong, let it be corrected by an amendment in the way which the Constitution designates. But let there be no change by usurpation; for though this, in one instance, may be the instrument of good, it is the customary weapon by which free governments are destroyed.[8]

Like Burke, most of the Founding Fathers, those who designed and supported the Constitution, believed that governments and societies should evolve with time. Except in rare cases of absolute despotism or destructive government, changes should be made slowly, deliberately, and through legal means. When the people ignore and usurp their constitutional systems of government, it puts society on a path to anarchy and chaos, eventually ending in tyranny.

The meaning of the American Revolution is still debated more than 200 years later. The ideological descendants of the angry mobs believe that the principles of liberty espoused in the Declaration of Independence are most important, whereas the followers of the Founding Fathers who wrote the Constitution believe that the political system established by the Constitution must be strictly maintained.

In fact, these two beliefs support each other. America needs the principles of liberty put forth by the Declaration of Independence and the limited government established by the Constitution. Liberty without government leads to anarchy while government without liberty leads to tyranny. Liberty and limited government must work together to promote "the perfect balance between liberty and power."[9]

Only by understanding the principles of the American Revolution set forth by the Declaration of Independence *and* following the system of government established by the Constitution can the American republic survive and flourish. Only by unifying the fierce spirit of the angry mobs with the prudence and wisdom of the Founding Fathers can the American people live in liberty, prosperity, and tranquility.

NOTES AND CITATIONS

PREFACE

1. Adams, *Familiar Letters of John Adams and His Wife Abigail Adams* 19.
2. Hamilton, Jay, and Madison, *The Federalist Papers* No. 1. Alexander Hamilton used these words to open the Federalist Papers.
3. Hamilton, Jay, and Madison, *The Federalist Papers* No. 14.

CHAPTER ONE
ANGRY MOBS
IN COLONIAL AMERICA

1. Paine, *Common Sense, Rights of Man, and Other Essential Writings of Thomas Paine* 24.
2. Paine, *Common Sense, Rights of Man, and Other Essential Writings of Thomas Paine* 25.
3. Butler, *Becoming America: The Revolution before 1776* 19.
4. Gordon, *An Empire of Wealth: The Epic History of American Economic Power* 52.
5. Perlmutter, *The Dynamics of American Ethnic, Religious, and Racial Group Life: An Interdisciplinary Overview* 9.
6. Butler, *Becoming America: The Revolution before 1776* 10.
7. Butler, *Becoming America: The Revolution before 1776* 33-34.
8. Franklin, *The Writings of Benjamin Franklin* 46-48.
9. Paine, *Common Sense, Rights of Man, and Other Essential Writings of Thomas Paine* 24.
10. Breen, *American Insurgents, American Patriots: The Revolution of the People* 26.
11. Atack and Passell, *A New Economic View of American History: from Colonial times to 1940* 68. Also Gordon, *An Empire of Wealth: The Epic History of American Economic Power* 54.
12. Johnson, *A History of the American People* 108.
13. This was the fourth French and Indian War, each of which accompanied a European war. In many respects, the American Revolution was the fifth French and Indian War and was part of a world war Britain fought against Spain and France. This time the American colonies fought against Britain instead of alongside it.
14. Smith, *An Inquiry into the Nature and Causes of the Wealth of Nations* 999-1000.
15. Smith, *An Inquiry into the Nature and Causes of the Wealth of Nations* 1025.
16. Wood, *The American Revolution: A History* 17 and Gordon, *An Empire of Wealth: The Epic History of American Economic Power* 54.

17. Gordon, *An Empire of Wealth: The Epic History of American Economic Power* 54.
18. Stauber, *The American Revolution: A Grand Mistake* 137.
19. Paine, *Common Sense, Rights of Man, and Other Essential Writings of Thomas Paine* 24.
20. Johnson, *A History of the American People* 133.
21. Schweikart, *The Entrepreneurial Adventure: A History of Business in the United States* 47 and DiLorenzo, *How Capitalism Saved America: The Untold History of Our Country, from the Pilgrims to the Present* 68.
22. Wood, *The American Revolution: A History* 28-29.
23. "The Declaration of Rights of the Stamp Act Congress, October 19, 1765."
24. Wood, *The American Revolution: A History* 28.
25. Wood, *The American Revolution: A History* 33 and Stauber, *The American Revolution: A Grand Mistake* 145.
26. Isaacson, *Benjamin Franklin: An American Life* 222-225.
27. Wood, *The American Revolution: A History* 29.
28. Wood, *The American Revolution: A History* 31.
29. The Albany Congress of 1754 was in cooperation with the British government and Indian nations.
30. Wood, *The American Revolution: A History* 27.
31. Stauber, *The American Revolution: A Grand Mistake* 143.
32. Schweikart, *The Entrepreneurial Adventure: A History of Business in the United States* 47.
33. *Collections of the Massachusetts Historical Society* 571.
34. Whately, *The Regulations Lately Made concerning the Colonies and the Taxes Imposed upon Them Considered* 109.
35. Wood, *The American Revolution: A History* 39-41.
36. Wood, *The American Revolution: A History* 31.
37. Smith, *An Inquiry into the Nature and Causes of the Wealth of Nations* 618.
38. Smith, *An Inquiry into the Nature and Causes of the Wealth of Nations* 1028.
39. Adams, *The Writings of Samuel Adams* Vol. 1, 185-186.
40. Wood, *The American Revolution: A History* 35.
41. Franklin, *The Works of Benjamin Franklin* Vol. 7, 467.
42. Commager and Morris, *The Spirit of 'Seventy-Six: The Story of the American Revolution as Told by Participants* 1 and Fleming, "Unlikely Victory," *What If?: The World's Foremost Military Historians Imagine What Might Have Been* 159.
43. Cobbett, *The Parliamentary History of England from the Earliest Period to the Year 1803* Vol. 17, 1280.
44. Breen, *American Insurgents, American Patriots: The Revolution of the People* 28.
45. Schweikart, *The Entrepreneurial Adventure: A History of Business in the United States* 39.
46. Schweikart, *The Entrepreneurial Adventure: A History of Business in the United States* 38.
47. Schweikart, *The Entrepreneurial Adventure: A History of Business in the United States* 38.
48. Johnson, *A History of the American People* 92 and Atack and Passell, *A New Economic View of American History: from Colonial times to 1940* 36.
49. DiLorenzo, *How Capitalism Saved America: The Untold History of Our Country, from the Pilgrims to the Present* 66.
50. Atack and Passell, *A New Economic View of American History: from Colonial times to 1940* 58.
51. Nettels, *The Emergence of a National Economy: 1775-1815* 235.

52. Atack and Passell, *A New Economic View of American History: from Colonial times to 1940* 58.

53. Atack and Passell, *A New Economic View of American History: from Colonial times to 1940* 59-62.

54. Thomas, "A Quantitative Approach to the Study of the Effects of British Imperial Policy upon Colonial Welfare: Some Preliminary Findings" 637-638.

55. McClelland, "The Cost to America of British Imperial Policy."

56. Atack and Passell, *A New Economic View of American History: from Colonial times to 1940* 62.

57. Roosevelt, *New York* 39-41.

58. Wood, *The American Revolution: A History* 57.

59. Gordon, *An Empire of Wealth: The Epic History of American Economic Power* 42-46.

60. Gordon, *An Empire of Wealth: The Epic History of American Economic Power* 47.

61. Atack and Passell, *A New Economic View of American History: from Colonial times to 1940* 65-66.

62. Franklin, *The Writings of Benjamin Franklin* Vol. 4, 420.

63. Smith, *An Inquiry into the Nature and Causes of the Wealth of Nations* 1024.

64. Smith, *An Inquiry into the Nature and Causes of the Wealth of Nations* 1020.

65. "The Declaration of Rights of the Stamp Act Congress, October 19, 1765."

66. Middleton, *Colonial America: A History, 1565 - 1776* 138.

67. Foner, *Give Me Liberty!: An American History* 100.

68. Wood, *The American Revolution: A History* 22.

69. Washington, *The Writings of George Washington* Ed. Jared Sparks, Vol. 2, 347.

70. Wood, *The American Revolution: A History* 22-23.

71. Wood, *The American Revolution: A History* 11.

72. Tocqueville, *Democracy in America and Two Essays on America* 47.

73. Henry, *Patrick Henry; Life, Correspondence and Speeches* Vol. 1, 40.

74. Washington, *The Writings of George Washington* Ed. John C. Fitzpatrick, Vol. 3, 224.

75. Stauber, *The American Revolution: A Grand Mistake* 160.

76. Stauber, *The American Revolution: A Grand Mistake* 153.

77. Tocqueville, *Democracy in America and Two Essays on America* 47.

78. Adams, *The Works of John Adams* Vol. 4, 393.

79. Butler, *Becoming America: The Revolution before 1776* 98.

80. Butler, *Becoming America: The Revolution before 1776* 98.

81. George III, *The Correspondence of King George the Third with Lord North from 1768 to 1783* Vol. 1, 215.

82. Nash, *The Forgotten Fifth: African Americans in the Age of Revolution* 26.

83. Hamilton, Jay, and Madison, *The Federalist Papers* No. 43.

84. Middleton, *Colonial America: A History, 1565 - 1776* 221.

85. Gordon, *An Empire of Wealth: The Epic History of American Economic Power* 31 and 51.

86. Butler, *Becoming America: The Revolution before 1776* 134-138; DiLorenzo, *How Capitalism Saved America: The Untold History of Our Country, from the Pilgrims to the Present* 62; and Gordon, *An Empire of Wealth: The Epic History of American Economic Power* 51.

87. Atack and Passell, *A New Economic View of American History: from Colonial times to 1940* 30-31.

88. Gordon, *An Empire of Wealth: The Epic History of American Economic Power* 49.

89. Johnson, *A History of the American People* 94.
90. Butler, *Becoming America: The Revolution before 1776* 111.
91. Butler, *Becoming America: The Revolution before 1776* 111.
92. Butler, *Becoming America: The Revolution before 1776* 82.
93. Osberg and Siddiq, "The Inequality Of Wealth in Britain's North American Colonies: The Importance Of The Relatively Poor" 161.
94. Gordon, *An Empire of Wealth: The Epic History of American Economic Power* 49.
95. Paine, *Common Sense, Rights of Man, and Other Essential Writings of Thomas Paine* 23, 30-31, 32-33, 44, and 54.
96. Paine, *Common Sense, Rights of Man, and Other Essential Writings of Thomas Paine* 40.
97. Adams, *The Works of John Adams* Vol. 10, 380-381.
98. Adams, *The Works of John Adams* Vol. 10, 283.
99. Adams, *The Works of John Adams* Vol. 10, 282.
100. Paine, *Common Sense, Rights of Man, and Other Essential Writings of Thomas Paine* 5 and 28.
101. Breen, *American Insurgents, American Patriots: The Revolution of the People* 11.
102. Burke, *The Works of the Right Hon. Edmund Burke* Vol. 1, 186.
103. Paine, *Common Sense, Rights of Man, and Other Essential Writings of Thomas Paine* 4 and 5.
104. Paine, *Common Sense, Rights of Man, and Other Essential Writings of Thomas Paine* 59-60.

CHAPTER TWO
FOUNDING FATHERS IN COLONIAL AMERICA

1. The Declaration of Independence concludes, "And for the support of this Declaration, with a firm reliance on the protection of Divine Providence, we mutually pledge to each other our Lives, our Fortunes, and our sacred Honor."
2. Tocqueville, *Democracy in America and Two Essays on America* 60.
3. Burke, *The Works of the Right Hon. Edmund Burke* Vol. 1, 186.
4. Frey, *Water from the Rock: Black Resistance in a Revolutionary Age* 133.
5. Hudelson, *Modern Political Philosophy* 37.
6. Douglass, *Oration Delivered in Corinthian Hall, Rochester* 10-11.
7. Smith, *An Inquiry into the Nature and Causes of the Wealth of Nations* 620.
8. Smith, *An Inquiry into the Nature and Causes of the Wealth of Nations* 630.
9. Thomas, "A Quantitative Approach to the Study of the Effects of British Imperial Policy upon Colonial Welfare: Some Preliminary Findings" 618 and Shepherd, "British America and the Atlantic Economy," *The Economy of Early America: The Revolutionary Period, 1763-1790* 25.
10. Shepherd, "British America and the Atlantic Economy," *The Economy of Early America: The Revolutionary Period, 1763-1790* 40.
11. Thomas, "A Quantitative Approach to the Study of the Effects of British Imperial Policy upon Colonial Welfare: Some Preliminary Findings" 619.

12. Shepherd, "British America and the Atlantic Economy," *The Economy of Early America: The Revolutionary Period, 1763-1790* 10.
13. Smith, *An Inquiry into the Nature and Causes of the Wealth of Nations* 629.
14. Smith, *An Inquiry into the Nature and Causes of the Wealth of Nations* 629.
15. Smith, *An Inquiry into the Nature and Causes of the Wealth of Nations* 631.
16. Atack and Passell, *A New Economic View of American History: From Colonial Times to 1940* 6.
17. Maier, *American Scripture: Making the Declaration of Independence* 28-29.
18. Hamilton, *The Papers of Alexander Hamilton* Vol. 1, 176.
19. Adams, *The Revolutionary Writings of John Adams* 131-132.
20. Adams, *The Works of John Adams* Vol. 1, 176.
21. Adams, *The Works of John Adams* Vol. 1, 218.
22. Adams, *The Works of John Adams* Vol. 9, 420.
23. Adams, *The Writings of Samuel Adams* Vol. 1, 5.
24. Adams, *The Writings of Samuel Adams* Vol. 2, 262.
25. Adams, *The Writings of Samuel Adams* Vol. 1, 239-240.
26. Adams, *The Writings of Samuel Adams* Vol. 2, 398.
27. Franklin, Franklin, and Duane, *Memoirs of Benjamin Franklin* 52-53.
28. Franklin, *The Works of Benjamin Franklin* Vol. 4, 156.
29. Franklin, *The Works of Benjamin Franklin* Vol. 4, 417.
30. Franklin, *The Works of Benjamin Franklin* Vol. 4, 417-418.
31. Franklin, *The Writings of Benjamin Franklin* Vol. 6, 179.
32. Carr, "William Pitt the Elder and the Avoidance of the American Revolution," *What Ifs? of American History: Eminent Historians Imagine What Might Have Been* 33.
33. Jefferson, *The Writings of Thomas Jefferson* Ed. Paul Leicester Ford, Vol. 1, 475.
34. Jefferson, *The Writings of Thomas Jefferson* Ed. Paul Leicester Ford, Vol. 1, 484.
35. Washington, *The Writings of George Washington* Ed. Jared Sparks, Vol. 2, 351.
36. Ellis, *His Excellency: George Washington* 61.
37. Washington, *The Writings of George Washington* Ed. Jared Sparks, Vol. 1, 137.
38. Paine, *Common Sense, Rights of Man, and Other Essential Writings of Thomas Paine* 32.
39. Ford, *Journals of the Continental Congress, 1774-1789* Vol. 1, 61-62.
40. Ford, *Journals of the Continental Congress, 1774-1789* Vol. 1, 82 and 89.
41. Ford, *Journals of the Continental Congress, 1774-1789* Vol. 1, 54.
42. Maier, *American Scripture: Making the Declaration of Independence* 3.
43. George III, *The Correspondence of King George the Third with Lord North from 1768 to 1783* Vol. 1, 215.
44. McClellan, *Liberty, Order, and Justice* 31-32.
45. Niles, *Centennial Offering. Republication of the Principles and Acts of the Revolution in America* 117-118.
46. Wood, *The American Revolution: A History* 53.
47. Maier, *American Scripture: Making the Declaration of Independence* 17-18.
48. Maier, *American Scripture: Making the Declaration of Independence* 10.
49. Washington, *The Writings of George Washington* Ed. Jared Sparks, Vol. 4, 113-115.
50. Swett, *History of Bunker Hill Battle: With a Plan* 50-51.
51. Ford, *Journals of the Continental Congress, 1774-1789* 109-110.
52. MacDonald, *Documentary Source Book of American History, 1606-1898* 189.

53. Force, *American Archives: Fourth Series. Containing a Documentary History of the English Colonies in North America* Vol. 6, 20.

54. Maier, *American Scripture: Making the Declaration of Independence* 25.

55. Stauber, *The American Revolution: A Grand Mistake* 155-156.

56. Ferling, *A Leap in the Dark: The Struggle to Create the American Republic* 138.

57. Adams, *The Works of John Adams* Vol. 2, 512.

58. Maier, *American Scripture: Making the Declaration of Independence* 18.

59. *American Historical Review* Vol. 1, 684-685.

60. Ferling, *A Leap in the Dark: The Struggle to Create the American Republic* 138.

61. Maier, *American Scripture: Making the Declaration of Independence* 217-234.

62. Maier, *American Scripture: Making the Declaration of Independence* 38.

63. Adams, *The Works of John Adams* Vol. 1, 219.

64. Maier, *American Scripture: Making the Declaration of Independence* 38.

65. Stauber, *The American Revolution: A Grand Mistake* 15. Also see the speech by William Pitt in the House of Lords on November 18, 1777 in Pitt, *Celebrated Speeches of Chatham, Burke, and Erskine* 36-38.

66. Stauber, *The American Revolution: A Grand Mistake* 172.

67. Maier, *American Scripture: Making the Declaration of Independence* 217-234.

68. Jefferson, *The Works of Thomas Jefferson* Vol. 12, 408-409.

69. Jefferson, *The Writings of Thomas Jefferson* Vol. 1, 335.

70. Washington, *The Writings of George Washington* Ed. Jared Sparks, Vol. 3, 343.

71. Ellis, *His Excellency: George Washington* 106.

72. Raphael, *A People's History of the American Revolution: How Common People Shaped the Fight for Independence* 66.

73. Foner, *Give Me Liberty!: An American History* 195.

74. Washington, *The Writings of George Washington* Ed. John C. Fitzpatrick, Vol. 6, 28.

75. Stauber, *The American Revolution: A Grand Mistake* 15.

76. Tocqueville, *Democracy in America and Two Essays on America* 755.

CHAPTER THREE
THE WAR FOR INDEPENDENCE

1. United States Declaration of Independence.

2. Nettels, *The Emergence of National Economy: 1775-1815* 34-35.

3. Nettels, *The Emergence of National Economy: 1775-1815* 34-35.

4. Wood, *The American Revolution: A History* 76.

5. Fleming, "Unlikely Victory," *What If?: The World's Foremost Military Historians Imagine What Might Have Been* 165.

6. Foner, *Give Me Liberty!: An American History* 195.

7. Fischer, *Washington's Crossing* 259.

8. Skousen, *The 5000 Year Leap: A Miracle That Changed the World* 20.

9. Fleming, "Unlikely Victory," *What If?: The World's Foremost Military Historians Imagine What Might Have Been* 175-178.

10. Marshall, *The Life of George Washington* Vol. 4, 348.

11. Fleming, "Unlikely Victory," *What If?: The World's Foremost Military Historians Imagine What Might Have Been* 179.
12. Mackesy, *The War for America: 1775-1783* 177-178.
13. Mackesy, *The War for America: 1775-1783* 215.
14. Stauber, *The American Revolution: A Grand Mistake* 164.
15. Raphael, *A People's History of the American Revolution: How Common People Shaped the Fight for Independence* 178-179.
16. Stauber, *The American Revolution: A Grand Mistake* 20.
17. Wood, *The American Revolution: A History* 113.
18. Johnson, *A History of the American People* 172.
19. Stauber, *The American Revolution: A Grand Mistake* 164.
20. Tiedemann, "Patriots by Default: Queens County, New York, and the British Army, 1776-1783" 36-37.
21. Ford, *Journals of the Continental Congress, 1774-1789* 46 and 123.
22. Stauber, *The American Revolution: A Grand Mistake* 189.
23. Paine, *Common Sense, Rights of Man, and Other Essential Writings of Thomas Paine* 34 and 60.
24. Howe, *The Narrative of Lieut. Gen. Sir William Howe* 39.
25. Shy, *A People Numerous and Armed: Reflections on the Military Struggle for American Independence* 23.
26. Fleming, "Unlikely Victory," *What If?: The World's Foremost Military Historians Imagine What Might Have Been* 175.
27. Phillips, *The Cousins' Wars: Religion, Politics, and the Triumph of Anglo-America* 162.
28. Gordon, *An Empire of Wealth: The Epic History of American Economic Power* 61.
29. Raphael, *A People's History of the American Revolution: How Common People Shaped the Fight for Independence* 168-170 and 198.
30. Frey, *Water from the Rock: Black Resistance in a Revolutionary Age* 133.
31. Reed, *Life and Correspondence of Joseph Reed* Vol. 2, 149-155 and Watson, *Annals of Philadelphia and Pennsylvania, in the Olden Time* Vol. 1, 425-427. There is some dispute as to how many men died in the riot, with estimates ranging from two to eight.
32. Nash, *The Forgotten Fifth: African Americans in the Age of Revolution* 67.
33. Paine, *Common Sense, Rights of Man, and Other Essential Writings of Thomas Paine* 39.
34. Nash, *The Forgotten Fifth: African Americans in the Age of Revolution* 26.
35. Quarles, *The Negro in the American Revolution* xxvii.
36. Nash, *The Forgotten Fifth: African Americans in the Age of Revolution* 8-10.
37. Raphael, *Founding Myths: Stories That Hide Our Patriotic Past* 185, 188-189, and 319-320.
38. Nash, *The Forgotten Fifth: African Americans in the Age of Revolution* 5-6 and Foner, *Give Me Liberty!: An American History* 225.
39. Jefferson, *The Writings of Thomas Jefferson* Ed. H. A. Washington, Vol. 2, 427.
40. Nash, *The Forgotten Fifth: African Americans in the Age of Revolution* 39.
41. In comparison, about 120,000 slaves fought in Rome's Third Servile War led by Spartacus, the most famous and generally believed to be the largest slave revolt in world history.
42. Nash, *The Forgotten Fifth: African Americans in the Age of Revolution* 35-41.
43. Adams and Adams, *Familiar Letters of John Adams and His Wife Abigail Adams* 41.

44. Nash, *The Forgotten Fifth: African Americans in the Age of Revolution* 126.
45. Wood, *The American Revolution: A History* 80-83.
46. Nettels, *The Emergence of National Economy: 1775-1815* 8-13.
47. Franklin, *The Writings of Benjamin Franklin* Vol. 7, 5.
48. Franklin, *The Writings of Benjamin Franklin* Vol. 7, 57.
49. Nettels, *The Emergence of National Economy: 1775-1815* 11.
50. Nettels, *The Emergence of National Economy: 1775-1815* 11.
51. Stauber, *The American Revolution: A Grand Mistake* 187.
52. Wood, *The American Revolution: A History* 84-85.
53. Paine, *Common Sense, Rights of Man, and Other Essential Writings of Thomas Paine* 77.
54. Fleming, "Unlikely Victory," *What If?: The World's Foremost Military Historians Imagine What Might Have Been* 162-163.
55. Washington, *The Writings of George Washington* Ed. Jared Sparks, Vol. 3, 341.
56. Reed, *Life and Correspondence of Joseph Reed* Vol. 1, 177.
57. Fleming, "Unlikely Victory," *What If?: The World's Foremost Military Historians Imagine What Might Have Been* 162-163 and Washington, *The Writings of George Washington* Ed. Jared Sparks, Vol. 3, 341.
58. Fleming, "Unlikely Victory," *What If?: The World's Foremost Military Historians Imagine What Might Have Been* 163-164.
59. Washington, *The Writings of George Washington* Ed. Jared Sparks, Vol. 7, 449.
60. Cowley, *What If?: The World's Foremost Military Historians Imagine What Might Have Been* 156.
61. Fleming, "Unlikely Victory," *What If?: The World's Foremost Military Historians Imagine What Might Have Been* 180-182.
62. Raphael, *Founding Myths: Stories That Hide Our Patriotic Past* 211.
63. Stauber, *The American Revolution: A Grand Mistake* 193.
64. Franklin, *Memoirs of Benjamin Franklin* Vol. 1, 501.
65. Gordon, *An Empire of Wealth: The Epic History of American Economic Power* 61-62.
66. Anderton, Barrett, and Bogue, *The Population of the United States* 6.
67. Anderton, Barrett, and Bogue, *The Population of the United States* 6.
68. Meyerson, *Liberty's Blueprint: How Madison and Hamilton Wrote the Federalist Papers, Defined the Constitution, and Made Democracy Safe for the World* 40 and Burrows and Wallace, *Gotham: A History of New York City to 1898* 258.
69. Meyerson, *Liberty's Blueprint: How Madison and Hamilton Wrote the Federalist Papers, Defined the Constitution, and Made Democracy Safe for the World* 40.
70. Shepherd, "British America and the Atlantic Economy," *The Economy of Early America: The Revolutionary Period, 1763-1790* 38, 40-41, and 25.
71. Atack and Passell, *A New Economic View of American History: From Colonial Times to 1940* 112-114.
72. Atack and Passell, *A New Economic View of American History: From Colonial Times to 1940* 114.
73. Atack and Passell, *A New Economic View of American History: From Colonial Times to 1940* 114-116 and Shepherd, "British America and the Atlantic Economy," *The Economy of Early America: The Revolutionary Period, 1763-1790* 27-32.
74. Butler, *Becoming America: The Revolution before 1776* 237.
75. Atack and Passell, *A New Economic View of American History: From Colonial Times to 1940* 8-14.

76. Commager and Morris, *The Spirit of 'Seventy-Six: The Story of the American Revolution as Told by Participants* 1295.

77. Schweikart, *The Entrepreneurial Adventure: A History of Business in the United States* 50.

CHAPTER FOUR
CHAOS IN THE CONFEDERATION

1. Wells, *Life and Public Services of Samuel Adams* Vol. 3, 175.

2. The Articles of Confederation.

3. Hamilton, *The Works of Alexander Hamilton* Ed. John C. Hamilton, Vol. 2, 222.

4. Wood, *The American Revolution: A History* 70-71.

5. Skousen, *The 5000 Year Leap: A Miracle That Changed the World* 20.

6. Gordon, *An Empire of Wealth: The Epic History of American Economic Power* 63.

7. Gordon, *An Empire of Wealth: The Epic History of American Economic Power* 60.

8. Raphael, *Founding Myths: Stories That Hide Our Patriotic Past* 88-92.

9. Franklin, *The Writings of Benjamin Franklin* Vol. 8, 645.

10. Nettels, *The Emergence of a National Economy: 1775-1815* 77 and 94.

11. Wood, *The American Revolution: A History* 146.

12. Madison, *The Writings of James Madison* 130.

13. Meyerson, *Liberty's Blueprint: How Madison and Hamilton Wrote the Federalist Papers, Defined the Constitution, and Made Democracy Safe for the World* 17-18.

14. Schweikart, *The Entrepreneurial Adventure: A History of Business in the United States* 50.

15. Atack and Passell, *A New Economic View of American History: From Colonial Times to 1940* 71-72 and Schweikart, *The Entrepreneurial Adventure: A History of Business in the United States* 50.

16. Washington, *The Writings of George Washington* Ed. Jared Sparks, Vol. 6, 228-229.

17. Nettels, *The Emergence of a National Economy: 1775-1815* 47-48.

18. Nettels, *The Emergence of a National Economy: 1775-1815* 231; Thomas, "A Quantitative Approach to the Study of the Effects of British Imperial Policy upon Colonial Welfare: Some Preliminary Findings" 618-619; and Shepherd, "British America and the Atlantic Economy," *The Economy of Early America: The Revolutionary Period, 1763-1790* 25.

19. Wood, *The American Revolution: A History* 115.

20. Atack and Passell, *A New Economic View of American History: From Colonial Times to 1940* 112-114 and Shepherd, "British America and the Atlantic Economy," *The Economy of Early America: The Revolutionary Period, 1763-1790* 38.

21. Wood, *The American Revolution: A History* 148-149.

22. Nettels, *The Emergence of a National Economy: 1775-1815* 62.

23. Atack and Passell, *A New Economic View of American History: From Colonial Times to 1940* 73.

24. Madison, *The Writings of James Madison* Vol. 2, 151.

25. Knox, *A History of Banking in the United States* 40.

26. Ferguson, "The Nationalists of 1781-1783 and the Economic Interpretation of the Constitution" 251.

27. Wood, *The American Revolution: A History* 148.
28. Wood, *The American Revolution: A History* 118-119.
29. Tocqueville, *Democracy in America and Two Essays on America* 131-132.
30. Hamilton, *The Works of Alexander Hamilton* Ed. John C. Hamilton, Vol. 1, 155-156.
31. This is the more dramatic telling of events. Others suggest that Washington took out his glasses and made his comment about growing gray and blind prior to his prepared remarks and that "the speech itself is anti-climactic." See Ellis, *His Excellency: George Washington* 144 and 299.
32. Sparks, *The Life of Gouverneur Morris: With Selections from His Correspondence and Miscellaneous Papers* Vol. 1, 251.
33. Ellis, *His Excellency: George Washington* 139.
34. Washington, *The Writings of George Washington* Ed. Jared Sparks, Vol. 9, 207. Shays' Rebellion could have come straight out of Plato's *Republic*. Plato writes, "And is it not true that in like manner a leader of the people who, getting control of a docile mob, does not withhold his hand from the shedding of tribal blood, but by the customary unjust accusations brings a citizen into court and assassinates him, blotting out a human life, and with unhallowed tongue and lips that have tasted kindred blood, banishes and slays and hints at the abolition of debts and the partition of lands." (Plato, *Republic* 565e-566a.)
35. Hamilton, Jay, and Madison *The Federalist Papers* No. 21.
36. Wood, *The American Revolution: A History* 152.
37. Gordon, *An Empire of Wealth: The Epic History of American Economic Power* 64-65.
38. Wood, *The American Revolution: A History* 152.
39. Wood, *The American Revolution: A History* 67-68 and 139-141.
40. Wood, *The American Revolution: A History* 98-99.
41. Tocqueville, *Democracy in America and Two Essays on America* 52.
42. Wood, *The American Revolution: A History* 143-144.
43. Tocqueville, *Democracy in America and Two Essays on America* 101.
44. Hamilton, Jay, and Madison *The Federalist Papers* No. 10.
45. Wood, *The American Revolution: A History* 160.
46. Shepherd, "British America and the Atlantic Economy," *The Economy of Early America: The Revolutionary Period, 1763-1790* 33.
47. Shepherd, "British America and the Atlantic Economy," *The Economy of Early America: The Revolutionary Period, 1763-1790* 35.
48. Wood, *The American Revolution: A History* 150.
49. Nettels, *The Emergence of a National Economy: 1775-1815* 69-75.
50. Madison, *The Writings of James Madison* Vol. 2, 228.
51. Sobran, "Foreword," *The Anti-Federalists: Selected Writings and Speeches* xxviii.
52. Hamilton, *The Papers of Alexander Hamilton* 32.
53. Hamilton, Jay, and Madison *The Federalist Papers* No. 5.
54. Stauber, *The American Revolution: A Grand Mistake* 121.
55. Foner, *Give Me Liberty!: An American History* 238.
56. Madison, *The Writings of James Madison* Vol. 2, 365-366.
57. Madison, *The Writings of James Madison* Vol. 5, 27.
58. Madison, *The Writings of James Madison* Vol. 2, 346.
59. Madison, *The Writings of James Madison* Vol. 5, 27.
60. Madison, *The Writings of James Madison* Vol. 4, 390.

61. Wood, *The American Revolution: A History* 88.
62. Paine, *Common Sense, Rights of Man, and Other Essential Writings of Thomas Paine* 26.
63. *The American Historical Review* Vol. 12, 77.
64. Gordon, *An Empire of Wealth: The Epic History of American Economic Power* 63.
65. Wood, *The American Revolution: A History* 149 and Gordon, *An Empire of Wealth: The Epic History of American Economic Power* 63. See also Nettels, *The Emergence of a National Economy: 1775-1815* 102.
66. Hamilton, Jay, and Madison *The Federalist Papers* No. 15.
67. Paine, *Common Sense, Rights of Man, and Other Essential Writings of Thomas Paine* 266.

CHAPTER FIVE

CREATING THE CONSTITUTION

1. Hamilton, Jay, and Madison, *The Federalist Papers* No. 1.
2. McClellan, *Liberty, Order, and Justice* 158-160.
3. Hamilton, Jay, and Madison, *The Federalist Papers* No. 1.
4. Hamilton, Jay, and Madison, *The Federalist Papers* No. 15.
5. Tocqueville, *Democracy in America and Two Essays on America* 292 and 807.
6. Wood, *The American Revolution: A History* 152-153 and 164.
7. Elliot, *The Debates in the Several State Conventions on the Adoption of the Federal Constitution* Vol. 1, 117.
8. Meyerson, *Liberty's Blueprint: How Madison and Hamilton Wrote the Federalist Papers, Defined the Constitution, and Made Democracy Safe for the World* xiii and 50.
9. Hamilton, Jay, and Madison, *The Federalist Papers* No. 15.
10. Jefferson, *The Writings of Thomas Jefferson* Ed. H. A. Washington, Vol. 2, 260.
11. Jefferson, *The Writings of Thomas Jefferson* Ed. H. A. Washington, Vol. 2, 260.
12. Madison, *The Debates in the Federal Convention of 1787: Which Framed the Constitution of the United States of America* 16.
13. Tocqueville, *Democracy in America and Two Essays on America* 132-133 and 178.
14. Foner, *Give Me Liberty!: An American History* 246; Best, "Our Constitutional Founders" *What Would The Founders Think?*; and Wood, *The American Revolution: A History* 153-154. Almost as notable were those who did not attend. John Adams and Thomas Jefferson were overseas, Anti-Federalists Patrick Henry and Richard Henry Lee refused to attend, Samuel Adams was ill, and John Jay's appointment was blocked by New York Governor George Clinton, an avid Anti-Federalist and one of the nation's most powerful politicians.
15. Madison, *The Debates in the Federal Convention of 1787: Which Framed the Constitution of the United States of America* 128.
16. *United States Constitution*, Preamble.
17. *United States Constitution*, Signatories.
18. Madison, *The Debates in the Federal Convention of 1787: Which Framed the Constitution of the United States of America* 180.
19. Hamilton, Jay, and Madison, *The Federalist Papers* No. 49.
20. Hamilton, Jay, and Madison, *The Federalist Papers* No. 46.

21. Hamilton, Jay, and Madison, *The Federalist Papers* No. 39.
22. Hamilton, Jay, and Madison, *The Federalist Papers* No. 51.
23. Hamilton, Jay, and Madison, *The Federalist Papers* No. 48.
24. Hamilton, Jay, and Madison, *The Federalist Papers* No. 18.
25. Jefferson, *The Writings of Thomas Jefferson* Ed. H. A. Washington, Vol. 4, 506.
26. Tocqueville, *Democracy in America and Two Essays on America* 68 and 807.
27. The Founding Fathers conducted intense studies of political history to help them found the new federal and state governments. They studied the great political thinkers, including Aristotle, Cicero, Cato, Hume, Montesquieu, and Locke, along with the classical histories of Plutarch, Livy, and Tacitus. (Lutz, *A Preface to American Political Theory* 136-138.) In *A Defence of the Constitutions of Government of the United States of America*, John Adams "examined twelve ancient democratic republics, three ancient aristocratic republics, and three ancient monarchical republics." (McClellan, *Liberty, Order, and Justice* 16.) In Federalist No. 63, James Madison examines the constitutions of Athens, Sparta, and Carthage. In Federalist No. 6, Alexander Hamilton writes that "Sparta, Athens, Rome, and Carthage were all republics" and evaluates how they, along with Venice, Holland, and Britain, suffered as a result of the many wars they fought.
28. Washington, *The Writings of George Washington* Ed. Jared Sparks, Vol. 9, 161.
29. Washington, *The Writings of George Washington* Ed. John C. Fitzpatrick, Vol. 29, 22-23.
30. Madison, *The Debates in the Federal Convention of 1787: Which Framed the Constitution of the United States of America* 65.
31. Hamilton, Jay, and Madison, *The Federalist Papers* No. 10.
32. Madison, *The Writings of James Madison* Vol. 2, 365-366.
33. Jefferson, *The Writings of Thomas Jefferson* Ed. H. A. Washington, Vol. 7, 2.
34. Hamilton, *The Works of Alexander Hamilton* Ed. John C. Hamilton, Vol. 2, 416-417.
35. Pellew, *American Statesmen: John Jay* 364.
36. Elliot, *The Debates in the Several State Conventions on the Adoption of the Federal Constitution* Vol. 2, 41.
37. Hamilton, *The Works of Alexander Hamilton* Vol. 2, 416.
38. Hamilton, Jay, and Madison, *The Federalist Papers* No. 11.
39. Hamilton, *The Works of Alexander Hamilton* Ed. Henry Cabot Lodge, Vol. 2, 51-52.
40. Tocqueville, *Democracy in America and Two Essays on America* 178.
41. Adams, *The Works of John Adams* Vol. 4, 403.
42. Hamilton, Jay, and Madison, *The Federalist Papers* No. 51.
43. Hamilton, Jay, and Madison, *The Federalist Papers* No. 44.
44. Hamilton, Jay, and Madison, *The Federalist Papers* No. 28.
45. Jefferson, *The Writings of Thomas Jefferson* Ed. H. A. Washington, Vol. 8, 390.
46. Madison, *The Writings of James Madison* Vol. 9, 232.
47. Hamilton, Jay, and Madison, *The Federalist Papers* No. 48.
48. Lutz, *A Preface to American Political Theory* 136-138.
49. Lutz, *A Preface to American Political Theory* 117.
50. Polybius, *The Histories* 6.18.
51. Montesquieu, *Considerations on the Causes of the Greatness of the Romans and Their Decline* 87.
52. Washington, *The Writings of George Washington* Ed. Jared Sparks, Vol. 12, 226.
53. Hamilton, Jay, and Madison, *The Federalist Papers* No. 39.

54. Hamilton, Jay, and Madison, *The Federalist Papers* No. 28.

55. Hamilton, Jay, and Madison, *The Federalist Papers* No. 51.

56. Hamilton, *The Works of Alexander Hamilton* Ed. John C. Hamilton, Vol. 2, 444.

57. Wilson, "Speech of October 6, 1787," Philadelphia, *Constitution Society.*

58. Hamilton, Jay, and Madison, *The Federalist Papers* No. 45.

59. Hamilton, Jay, and Madison, *The Federalist Papers* No. 17.

60. Hamilton, Jay, and Madison, *The Federalist Papers* No. 85.

61. Madison, *The Writings of James Madison* Vol. 4, 390.

62. Tocqueville, *Democracy in America and Two Essays on America* 133.

63. Tocqueville, *Democracy in America and Two Essays on America* 167.

64. Tocqueville, *Democracy in America and Two Essays on America* 184.

65. "Government Spending Chart in United States," *Government Spending in United States* <www.usgovernmentspending.com/charts.html>.

66. Washington, *The Writings of George Washington* Ed. Jared Sparks, Vol. 9, 511.

67. Hamilton, Jay, and Madison, *The Federalist Papers* No. 47.

68. Hamilton, Jay, and Madison, *The Federalist Papers* No. 48.

69. Hamilton, Jay, and Madison, *The Federalist Papers* No. 51.

70. Tocqueville, *Democracy in America and Two Essays on America* 23.

71. A second amendment process is written into the Constitution wherein two-thirds of the states call a convention to propose amendments instead of Congress doing so. This method has never been tried.

72. Nash, *The Forgotten Fifth: African Americans in the Age of Revolution* 103.

73. Nash, *The Forgotten Fifth: African Americans in the Age of Revolution* 76-79.

74. Madison, *The Debates in the Federal Convention of 1787: Which Framed the Constitution of the United States of America* 195.

75. Madison, *The Debates in the Federal Convention of 1787: Which Framed the Constitution of the United States of America* 65.

76. Foner, *Give Me Liberty!: An American History* 228.

77. Nash, *The Forgotten Fifth: African Americans in the Age of Revolution* 132, 139-142, and 163.

78. Jefferson, *The Writings of Thomas Jefferson* Ed. H. A. Washington, Vol. 1, 23-24.

79. Atack and Passell, *A New Economic View of American History: From Colonial Times to 1940* 51.

80. Madison, *The Writings of James Madison* Vol. 8, 442.

81. Nash, *The Forgotten Fifth: African Americans in the Age of Revolution* 109.

82. Elliot, *The Debates in the Several State Conventions on the Adoption of the Federal Constitution* Vol.4, 299.

83. Nash, *The Forgotten Fifth: African Americans in the Age of Revolution* 82-84.

84. Meese, *The Heritage Guide to the Constitution* 150.

85. Meese, *The Heritage Guide to the Constitution* 275.

86. Atack and Passell, *A New Economic View of American History: From Colonial Times to 1940* 358.

87. Wood, *The American Revolution: A History* 128.

88. Nash, *The Forgotten Fifth: African Americans in the Age of Revolution* 105.

89. Nettels, *The Emergence of a National Economy: 1775-1815* 184 and 204.

90. Gordon, *An Empire of Wealth: The Epic History of American Economic Power* 83-84.

91. Nettels, *The Emergence of a National Economy: 1775-1815* 201.

92. Foner, *Give Me Liberty!: An American History* 379.

93. Schweikart, *The Entrepreneurial Adventure: A History of Business in the United States* 72.

94. Nettels, *The Emergence of a National Economy: 1775-1815* 192.

95. Gordon, *An Empire of Wealth: The Epic History of American Economic Power* 87.

96. Nettels, *The Emergence of a National Economy: 1775-1815* 137-138.

97. Atack and Passell, *A New Economic View of American History: From Colonial Times to 1940* 522-523.

98. Atack and Passell, *A New Economic View of American History: From Colonial Times to 1940* 13.

99. Nettels, *The Emergence of a National Economy: 1775-1815* 187.

100. Foner, *Give Me Liberty!: An American History* 379.

101. Atack and Passell, *A New Economic View of American History: From Colonial Times to 1940* 359-363.

102. See Nash, *The Forgotten Fifth: African Americans in the Age of Revolution* Chapter 3.

103. Stauber, *The American Revolution: A Grand Mistake* 24.

104. Fleming, *Duel: Alexander Hamilton, Aaron Burr, and the Future of America* 141.

105. Stauber, *The American Revolution: A Grand Mistake* 26.

106. Foner, *Give Me Liberty!: An American History* 127 and 136.

107. Wood, *The American Revolution: A History* 127.

108. Madison, *The Debates in the Federal Convention of 1787: Which Framed the Constitution of the United States of America* 469.

109. Douglass, *Oration Delivered in Corinthian Hall, Rochester* 36-37.

110. Hamilton, Jay, and Madison, *The Federalist Papers* No. 54.

111. Jefferson, *The Writings of Thomas Jefferson* Ed. H. A. Washington, Vol. 2, 260.

112. Jefferson, *The Writings of Thomas Jefferson* Ed. H. A. Washington, Vol. 2, 318.

113. Meyerson, *Liberty's Blueprint: How Madison and Hamilton Wrote the Federalist Papers, Defined the Constitution, and Made Democracy Safe for the World* 104.

114. Ford, *Essays on the Constitution of the United States, Published during Its Discussion by the People, 1787-1788* 68.

115. Sobran, "Foreword," *The Anti-Federalists: Selected Writings and Speeches* xxix-xxx.

116. For ratification dates and votes, see "Ratification Dates and Votes," *The U.S. Constitution Online*, USConstitution.net.

117. Meyerson, *Liberty's Blueprint: How Madison and Hamilton Wrote the Federalist Papers, Defined the Constitution, and Made Democracy Safe for the World* 89.

118. Washington, *The Writings of George Washington* Ed. Jared Sparks, Vol. 9, 352.

119. Jefferson, *The Writings of Thomas Jefferson* Ed. H. A. Washington, Vol. 2, 506.

120. Marshall, *The Life of George Washington* Vol. 5, 132.

121. Meyerson, *Liberty's Blueprint: How Madison and Hamilton Wrote the Federalist Papers, Defined the Constitution, and Made Democracy Safe for the World* 77.

122. Meyerson, *Liberty's Blueprint: How Madison and Hamilton Wrote the Federalist Papers, Defined the Constitution, and Made Democracy Safe for the World* 89-90.

123. Foner, *Give Me Liberty!: An American History* 254.

124. Meyerson, *Liberty's Blueprint: How Madison and Hamilton Wrote the Federalist Papers, Defined the Constitution, and Made Democracy Safe for the World* 89.

125. Foner, *Give Me Liberty!: An American History* 254.

126. Hamilton, *The Works of Alexander Hamilton* Vol. 1, 403.

127. Hamilton, Jay, and Madison, *The Federalist Papers* No. 11.

128. Tocqueville, *Democracy in America and Two Essays on America* 181.
129. Washington, *The Writings of George Washington* Ed. John C. Fitzpatrick, Vol. 29, 411.
130. Madison, *The Debates in the Federal Convention of 1787: Which Framed the Constitution of the United States of America* 578.
131. Wilson, "Speech of October 6, 1787," Philadelphia, *Constitution Society*.
132. Washington, *The Writings of George Washington* Ed. John C. Fitzpatrick, Vol. 30, 73.
133. Hamilton, Jay, and Madison, *The Federalist Papers* No. 85.
134. Hamilton, *The Works of Alexander Hamilton* Ed. Henry Cabot Lodge, Vol. 2, 51-52.
135. Adams, *The Works of John Adams* Vol. 10, 282.
136. Hamilton, Jay, and Madison, *The Federalist Papers* No. 14.
137. Wilson, *The Works of James Wilson* 530.
138. Jefferson, *The Writings of Thomas Jefferson* Ed. H. A. Washington, Vol. 3, 12.
139. Jay, *The Correspondence and Public Papers of John Jay* Vol. 1, 161.
140. Adams, *The Works of John Adams* Vol. 6, 220.
141. Webster, *Newly Discovered Fourth of July Oration* 14.
142. "Washington and the Constitution," *The Literary World* 20.7 (March 1889), 106.
143. Hamilton, Jay, and Madison, *The Federalist Papers* No. 38.
144. Montesquieu, *The Spirit of Laws* 229.
145. Polybius, *The Histories* 6.10.13-14.
146. Hamilton, Jay, and Madison, *The Federalist Papers* No. 1.
147. Lutz, *A Preface to American Political Theory* 117 and 136-138.
148. McMaster and Stone, *Pennsylvania and the Federal Constitution, 1787-1788* 420.
149. Washington, *The Writings of George Washington* Ed. John C. Fitzpatrick, Vol. 30, 292.
150. Hamilton, Jay, and Madison, *The Federalist Papers* No. 37.
151. Madison, *The Writings of James Madison* Vol. 9, 357.
152. Paine, *Common Sense, Rights of Man, and Other Essential Writings of Thomas Paine* 59-60.
153. Hamilton, Jay, and Madison, *The Federalist Papers* No. 11.
154. Hamilton, Jay, and Madison, *The Federalist Papers* No. 1.
155. Hamilton, Jay, and Madison, *The Federalist Papers* No. 14.
156. Madison, *The Writings of James Madison* Vol. 9, 357.
157. Jefferson, *The Writings of Thomas Jefferson* Ed. H. A. Washington, Vol. 8, 8.
158. Jefferson, *The Writings of Thomas Jefferson* Ed. Paul Leicester Ford, Vol. 8, 8.
159. Webster, *Newly Discovered Fourth of July Oration* 14.
160. Jefferson, *The Writings of Thomas Jefferson* Ed. H. A. Washington, Vol. 8, 8.
161. Franklin, *The Writings of Benjamin Franklin* Ed. Albert Henry Smyth, Vol. 10, 69.

CHAPTER SIX
A REPUBLIC, IF YOU CAN KEEP IT.

1. *American Historical Review* Vol. 11, 618. Punctuation according to Platt, *Respectfully Quoted: a Dictionary of Quotations* 299.
2. Hamilton, *The Works of Alexander Hamilton* Ed. Henry Cabot Lodge, Vol. 2, 51-52.
3. Gordon, *An Empire of Wealth: The Epic History of American Economic Power* 68.

4. Jefferson, *The Writings of Thomas Jefferson* Ed. H. A. Washington, Vol. 3, 363 and Vol. 4, 406. See also O'Brien, *First in Peace: How George Washington Set the Course for America* 57.

5. Ellis, *His Excellency: George Washington* 225.

6. Ward, Prothero, and Leathes, *The Cambridge Modern History.* 237.

7. McClellan, *Liberty, Order, and Justice* 406.

8. Preamble to the Bill of Rights.

9. Hamilton, Jay, and Madison, *The Federalist Papers* No. 84.

10. Madison, *The Writings of James Madison* Vol. 5, 271-272.

11. Madison, *The Writings of James Madison* Vol. 5, 384-385.

12. United States Constitution, Article 1 Section 8.

13. Hamilton, Jay, and Madison, *The Federalist Papers* No. 44.

14. Washington, *The Writings of George Washington* Ed. Jared Sparks, Vol. 12, 33.

15. Washington, *The Writings of George Washington* Ed. Jared Sparks, Vol. 12, 41.

16. Jefferson, *The Writings of Thomas Jefferson* Ed. H. A. Washington, Vol. 7, 19.

17. Atack and Passell, *A New Economic View of American History: From Colonial Times to 1940* 127.

18. Atack and Passell, *A New Economic View of American History: From Colonial Times to 1940* 127.

19. Atack and Passell, *A New Economic View of American History: From Colonial Times to 1940* 127 and Johnson, *A History of the American People* 213.

20. Nettels, *The Emergence of a National Economy: 1775-1815* 111.

21. Elliott, *The Tariff Controversy in the United States, 1789-1833* 68.

22. Nettels, *The Emergence of a National Economy: 1775-1815* 109 and 111.

23. Hamilton, *The Works of Alexander Hamilton* Ed. John C. Hamilton, Vol. 3, 5.

24. Hamilton, *The Works of Alexander Hamilton* Ed. John C. Hamilton, Vol. 1, 125.

25. Hamilton, *The Works of Alexander Hamilton* Ed. John C. Hamilton, Vol. 3, 8.

26. Madison, *The Writings of James Madison* Vol. 1, 459.

27. Meyerson, *Liberty's Blueprint: How Madison and Hamilton Wrote the Federalist Papers, Defined the Constitution, and Made Democracy Safe for the World* 114.

28. Hamilton, *The Works of Alexander Hamilton* Ed. Henry Cabot Lodge, Vol. 8, 260.

29. Hamilton, *The Papers of Alexander Hamilton* Vol. 19, 62.

30. Hamilton, *The Works of Alexander Hamilton* Ed. John C. Hamilton, Vol. 3, 4.

31. Ferguson, "The Nationalists of 1781-1783 and the Economic Interpretation of the Constitution" 251.

32. Madison, *The Debates in the Federal Convention of 1787: Which Framed the Constitution of the United States of America* 255 and 421-422.

33. Madison, *The Debates in the Federal Convention of 1787: Which Framed the Constitution of the United States of America* 421-422.

34. Hamilton, *The Works of Alexander Hamilton* Ed. John C. Hamilton, Vol. 1, 257.

35. Hamilton, *The Works of Alexander Hamilton* Ed. John C. Hamilton, Vol. 3, 5.

36. Meyerson, *Liberty's Blueprint: How Madison and Hamilton Wrote the Federalist Papers, Defined the Constitution, and Made Democracy Safe for the World* 115 and 123.

37. Jefferson, *The Writings of Thomas Jefferson* Ed. Paul Leicester Ford, Vol. 6, 239.

38. Hamilton, *The Works of Alexander Hamilton* Ed. John C. Hamilton, Vol. 3, 503.

39. Jefferson, *The Writings of Thomas Jefferson* Ed. H. A. Washington, Vol. 3, 460.

40. Hamilton, *The Works of Alexander Hamilton* Ed. John C. Hamilton, Vol.1, 257.

41. Chernow, *Alexander Hamilton* 347.

42. Atack and Passell, *A New Economic View of American History: From Colonial Times to 1940* 92.

43. Atack and Passell, *A New Economic View of American History: From Colonial Times to 1940* 651; Gordon, *An Empire of Wealth: The Epic History of American Economic Power* 76-79; and Schweikart, *The Entrepreneurial Adventure: A History of Business in the United States* 82.

44. Hamilton, Jay, and Madison, *The Federalist Papers* No. 44.

45. Jefferson, *The Writings of Thomas Jefferson* Ed. H. A. Washington, Vol. 6, 305.

46. Adams, *The Works of John Adams* Ed. Charles Francis Adams, Vol. 9, 610.

47. Atack and Passell, *A New Economic View of American History: From Colonial Times to 1940* 92.

48. Hamilton, Jay, and Madison, *The Federalist Papers* No. 44.

49. Hamilton, *The Works of Alexander Hamilton* Ed. John C. Hamilton, Vol. 3, 433.

50. Hamilton, *The Works of Alexander Hamilton* Ed. John C. Hamilton, Vol. 4, 110.

51. Hamilton, *The Works of Alexander Hamilton* Ed. John C. Hamilton, Vol. 4, 113.

52. Grossman, *Unsettled Account: The Evolution of Banking in the Industrialized World since 1800* 223.

53. McCulloch v. Maryland.

54. Lane, "For "A Positive Profit": The Federal Investment in the First Bank of the United States, 1792-1802"; Clark, Craig, and Wilson, *A History of Public Sector Pensions in the United States* 70; and Nettels, *The Emergence of a National Economy: 1775-1815* 118 and 120.

55. Nettels, *The Emergence of a National Economy: 1775-1815* 295.

56. Atack and Passell, *A New Economic View of American History: From Colonial Times to 1940* 92.

57. Nettels, *The Emergence of a National Economy: 1775-1815* 295.

58. Gordon, *An Empire of Wealth: The Epic History of American Economic Power* 79 and Nettels, *The Emergence of a National Economy: 1775-1815* 338-340.

59. Nettels, *The Emergence of a National Economy: 1775-1815* 338 and Schweikart, *The Entrepreneurial Adventure: A History of Business in the United States* 81.

60. Gordon, *An Empire of Wealth: The Epic History of American Economic Power* 79.

61. Nettels, *The Emergence of a National Economy: 1775-1815* 316.

62. Nettels, *The Emergence of a National Economy: 1775-1815* 116-117.

63. Debt data from Nettels, *The Emergence of a National Economy: 1775-1815* 384. Population data from Anderton, Barrett, and Bogue, *The Population of the United States* 6. Calculated 1791 population based on 1790 population and average population growth during that decade.

64. Debt data from Nettels, *The Emergence of a National Economy: 1775-1815* 384. Gross domestic product data from "United States Federal State and Local Government Spending," *Government Spending in the United States of America*. GDP data is first available for the year 1792.

65. Washington, *The Writings of George Washington* Ed. Jared Sparks, Vol. 10, 172.

66. Gordon, *An Empire of Wealth: The Epic History of American Economic Power* 75.

67. Hamilton, *The Works of Alexander Hamilton* Ed. John C. Hamilton, Vol. 3, 526.

68. Atack and Passell, *A New Economic View of American History: From Colonial Times to 1940* 112 and 116.
69. Washington, *The Writings of George Washington* Ed. Jared Sparks, Vol. 10, 169 and 170-171.
70. Nettels, *The Emergence of a National Economy: 1775-1815* 234-237 and 242.
71. Nettels, *The Emergence of a National Economy: 1775-1815* 234-239 and 267.
72. Nettels, *The Emergence of a National Economy: 1775-1815* 116.
73. Washington, *The Writings of George Washington* Ed. Jared Sparks, Vol. 12, 44-45.
74. Washington, *The Writings of George Washington* Ed. Jared Sparks, Vol. 10, 444.
75. Jefferson, *The Writings of Thomas Jefferson* Ed. H. A. Washington, Vol. 2, 209.
76. Jefferson, *The Writings of Thomas Jefferson* Ed. H. A. Washington, Vol. 3, 502.
77. Hitchens, "Cruiser," Foreword, *First in Peace: How George Washington Set the Course for America* 14; O'Brien, *First in Peace: How George Washington Set the Course for America* 21-22 and 138; and *American State Papers: Documents, Legislative and Executive of the Congress of the United States* Vol. 1, 398.
78. O'Brien, *First in Peace: How George Washington Set the Course for America* 60.
79. O'Brien, *First in Peace: How George Washington Set the Course for America* 82.
80. See O'Brien, *First in Peace: How George Washington Set the Course for America* 74-121 for more about Genet's activities in the United States.
81. Meyerson, *Liberty's Blueprint: How Madison and Hamilton Wrote the Federalist Papers, Defined the Constitution, and Made Democracy Safe for the World* 126. See also Hitchens, "Cruiser," Foreword, *First in Peace: How George Washington Set the Course for America* 9.
82. O'Brien, *First in Peace: How George Washington Set the Course for America* 97-98 and 115.
83. McClellan, *Liberty, Order, and Justice* 492-493.
84. Hamilton, *The Papers of Alexander Hamilton* Vol. 25, 257. As Jefferson turned out to be a great President while Burr was later accused of and indicted for treason, Hamilton appears to have been correct in his assessment. Of course, Hamilton did not live to see Burr's treason because Burr shot and killed him in a duel in 1804.
85. Jefferson, *The Writings of Thomas Jefferson* Ed. H. A. Washington, Vol. 8, 2-3.
86. Hamilton, *Reminiscences of James A. Hamilton; Or, Men and Events, at Home and Abroad, during Three Quarters of a Century* 23.
87. Jefferson, *The Writings of Thomas Jefferson* Ed. Paul Leicester Ford, Vol. 8, 127.
88. Nettels, *The Emergence of a National Economy: 1775-1815* 338-340.
89. Chernow, *Alexander Hamilton* 646.
90. Nettels, *The Emergence of a National Economy: 1775-1815* 319, 384, 385, and 386.
91. Nettels, *The Emergence of a National Economy: 1775-1815* 301, 333-334, and 338.
92. Nettels, *The Emergence of a National Economy: 1775-1815* 340.
93. Schweikart, *The Entrepreneurial Adventure: A History of Business in the United States* 82.
94. "United States Federal State and Local Government Spending," *Government Spending in the United States of America.*
95. "United States Federal State and Local Government Spending," *Government Spending in the United States of America.*
96. Atack and Passell, *A New Economic View of American History: From Colonial Times to 1940* 93-94.

97. Atack and Passell, *A New Economic View of American History: From Colonial Times to 1940* 95.

98. Johnson, *A History of the American People* 355-356.

99. Atack and Passell, *A New Economic View of American History: From Colonial Times to 1940* 99 and 102.

100. Gordon, *An Empire of Wealth: The Epic History of American Economic Power* 128.

101. Atack and Passell, *A New Economic View of American History: From Colonial Times to 1940* 95-97.

102. Atack and Passell, *A New Economic View of American History: From Colonial Times to 1940* 96-102 and Gordon, *An Empire of Wealth: The Epic History of American Economic Power* 130.

103. Gordon, *An Empire of Wealth: The Epic History of American Economic Power* 130 and 179.

104. Johnson, *A History of the American People* 357.

105. Wallis, "Sovereign Default and Repudiation: The Emerging-Market Debt Crisis in U.S. States, 1839-1843" 33.

106. Johnson, *A History of the American People* 357.

107. "United States Federal State and Local Government Spending," *Government Spending in the United States of America.*

108. Atack and Passell, *A New Economic View of American History: From Colonial Times to 1940* 99 and 103-108.

109. Nettels, *The Emergence of a National Economy: 1775-1815* 385 and 396.

110. Atack and Passell, *A New Economic View of American History: From Colonial Times to 1940* 117-121; Gordon, *An Empire of Wealth: The Epic History of American Economic Power* 94-95; and Nettels, *The Emergence of a National Economy: 1775-1815* 396.

111. Atack and Passell, *A New Economic View of American History: From Colonial Times to 1940* 122.

112. Nettels, *The Emergence of a National Economy: 1775-1815* 340.

113. Nettels, *The Emergence of a National Economy: 1775-1815* 340.

114. Jefferson, *The Writings of Thomas Jefferson* Ed. H. A. Washington, Vol. 6, 521-523.

115. Atack and Passell, *A New Economic View of American History: From Colonial Times to 1940* 122.

116. Fleming, *Duel: Alexander Hamilton, Aaron Burr, and the Future of America* 141.

117. Jefferson, *The Writings of Thomas Jefferson* Ed. H. A. Washington, Vol. 4, 500-501.

118. Atack and Passell, *A New Economic View of American History: From Colonial Times to 1940* 275.

119. Nettels, *The Emergence of a National Economy: 1775-1815* 167.

120. Atack and Passell, *A New Economic View of American History: From Colonial Times to 1940* 8-15.

121. Hamilton, *The Works of Alexander Hamilton* Ed. John C. Hamilton, Vol. 3, 123.

122. Atack and Passell, *A New Economic View of American History: From Colonial Times to 1940* 8.

123. Atack and Passell, *A New Economic View of American History: From Colonial Times to 1940* 164.

124. Atack and Passell, *A New Economic View of American History: From Colonial Times to 1940* 156-159.

125. Atack and Passell, *A New Economic View of American History: From Colonial Times to 1940* 159-160.
126. Nettels, *The Emergence of a National Economy: 1775-1815* 261 and 292.
127. Atack and Passell, *A New Economic View of American History: From Colonial Times to 1940* 171.
128. Atack and Passell, *A New Economic View of American History: From Colonial Times to 1940* 153-155.
129. Atack and Passell, *A New Economic View of American History: From Colonial Times to 1940* 429.
130. Atack and Passell, *A New Economic View of American History: From Colonial Times to 1940* 437-438.
131. Atack and Passell, *A New Economic View of American History: From Colonial Times to 1940* 145, 152, and 161.
132. Atack and Passell, *A New Economic View of American History: From Colonial Times to 1940* 178.
133. Hamilton, *The Works of Alexander Hamilton* Ed. Henry Cabot Lodge, Vol. 2, 51-52.
134. Washington, *The Writings of George Washington* Ed. Jared Sparks, Vol. 10, 169.

EPILOGUE

1. Paine, *Common Sense, Rights of Man, and Other Essential Writings of Thomas Paine* 138.
2. Jefferson, *The Writings of Thomas Jefferson* Ed. H. A. Washington, Vol. 2, 318-319.
3. Jefferson, *The Writings of Thomas Jefferson* Ed. H. A. Washington, Vol. 3, 502.
4. Jefferson, *The Writings of Thomas Jefferson* Ed. H. A. Washington, Vol. 7, 14-16.
5. Burke, *The Works of the Right Hon. Edmund Burke* Vol. 1, 417.
6. Jefferson, *The Writings of Thomas Jefferson* Ed. H. A. Washington, Vol. 6, 136-137.
7. Hamilton, *The Works of Alexander Hamilton* Ed. John C. Hamilton, Vol. 1, 465.
8. Washington, *The Writings of George Washington* Ed. John C. Fitzpatrick, Vol. 35, 228.
9. Hamilton, *The Works of Alexander Hamilton* Ed. Henry Cabot Lodge, Vol. 2, 51-52.

BIBLIOGRAPHY

Adams, John. *The Revolutionary Writings of John Adams*. Ed. C. Bradley. Thompson. Indianapolis: Liberty Fund, 2000.

Adams, John. *The Works of John Adams*. Ed. Charles Francis Adams. Boston: Little, Brown and Co., 1856.

Adams, John, and Abigail Adams. *Familiar Letters of John Adams and His Wife Abigail Adams*. Ed. Charles Francis Adams. New York: Hurd and Houghton, 1876.

Adams, John, Samuel Adams, and James Warren. *Warren-Adams Letters, Being Chiefly a Correspondence among John Adams, Samuel Adams, and James Warren*. Boston: Massachusetts Historical Society, 1917.

Adams, Samuel. *The Writings of Samuel Adams*. Ed. Harry Alonzo Cushing. New York: G.P. Putnam's Sons, 1904.

American Historical Review. New York: Macmillan, 1896-1907.

American State Papers: Documents, Legislative and Executive of the Congress of the United States. Washington: Gales and Seaton, 1832.

Anderton, Douglas L., Richard E. Barrett, and Donald J. Bogue. *The Population of the United States*. New York: Free Press, 1997.

Atack, Jeremy, and Peter Passell. *A New Economic View of American History: From Colonial Times to 1940*. New York: W.W. Norton, 1994.

Best, James D. "Our Constitutional Founders." *What Would The Founders Think?* 4 Nov. 2010.

Breen, T. H. *American Insurgents, American Patriots: The Revolution of the People*. New York: Hill and Wang, 2010.

Burke, Edmund. *The Works of the Right Hon. Edmund Burke*. Ed. Henry Rogers. London: S. Holdsworth, 1837.

Burrows, Edwin G. and Mike Wallace. *Gotham: A History of New York City to 1898*. New York: Oxford University Press, 1999.

Butler, Jon. *Becoming America: The Revolution before 1776*. Cambridge, MA: Harvard University Press, 2000.

Carr, Caleb. "William Pitt the Elder and the Avoidance of the American Revolution." *What Ifs? of American History: Eminent Historians Imagine What Might Have Been*. Ed. Robert Cowley. New York: G.P. Putnam's Sons, 2003. 19-42.

Chamberlain, Mellen, and John Adams. *John Adams the Statesman of the American Revolution*. Boston and New York: Houghton, Mifflin and Company, 1898.

Chernow, Ron. *Alexander Hamilton*. New York: Penguin, 2004.

Clark, Robert L., Lee A. Craig, and Jack W. Wilson. *A History of Public Sector Pensions in the United States*. Philadelphia: University of Pennsylvania, 2003.

Collections of the Massachusetts Historical Society. Vol. X. Boston: Massachusetts Historical Society, 1871.

Commager, Henry Steele, and Richard B. Morris. *The Spirit of 'Seventy-Six: The Story of the American Revolution as Told by Participants*. New York: Da Capo, 1995.

Cobbett, William. *The Parliamentary History of England from the Earliest Period to the Year 1803*. London: T. C. Hansard, 1813.

Cowley, Robert, ed. *What If?: The World's Foremost Military Historians Imagine What Might Have Been*. New York: Berkley, 2000.

Cowley, Robert, ed. *What Ifs? of American History: Eminent Historians Imagine What Might Have Been*. New York: G.P. Putnam's Sons, 2003.

DiLorenzo, Thomas J. *How Capitalism Saved America: The Untold History of Our Country, from the Pilgrims to the Present*. New York: Three Rivers, 2004.

Douglass, Frederick. *Oration Delivered in Corinthian Hall, Rochester*. Rochester: Lee, Mann & Co., 1852.

Elliot, Jonathan, ed. *The Debates in the Several State Conventions on the Adoption of the Federal Constitution*. 2nd ed. Washington, 1836.

Elliott, Orrin Leslie. *The Tariff Controversy in the United States, 1789-1833*. Palo Alto: Leland Stanford Junior University, 1892.

Ellis, Joseph J. *His Excellency: George Washington*. New York: Alfred A. Knopf, 2004.

Ferguson, E. James. "The Nationalists of 1781-1783 and the Economic Interpretation of the Constitution." *The Journal of American History* 56.2 (Sep. 1969): 241-61.

Ferling, John E. *A Leap in the Dark: The Struggle to Create the American Republic*. New York: Oxford University Press, 2003.

Fischer, David Hackett. *Washington's Crossing*. Oxford, England: Oxford University Press, 2004.

Fleming, Thomas. *Duel: Alexander Hamilton, Aaron Burr, and the Future of America*. New York, NY: Basic Books, 1999.

Fleming, Thomas. "Unlikely Victory." *What If?: The World's Foremost Military Historians Imagine What Might Have Been*. Ed. Robert Cowley. New York: Berkley, 2000. 155-86.

Foner, Eric. *Give Me Liberty!: An American History*. Volume 1. Second Edition. New York: W.W. Norton, 2009.

Force, Peter, ed. *American Archives: Fourth Series. Containing a Documentary History of the English Colonies in North America*. Washington: Clarke & Force, 1846.

Ford, Paul Leicester, ed. *Essays on the Constitution of the United States, Published during Its Discussion by the People, 1787-1788*. Brooklyn, NY: Historical Printing Club, 1892.

Ford, Worthington Chauncey, ed. *Journals of the Continental Congress, 1774-1789*. Washington: Government Printing Office, 1904-1906.

Franklin, Benjamin. *The Works of Benjamin Franklin*. Ed. Jared Sparks. Philadelphia: Childs & Peterson, 1840.

Franklin, Benjamin. *The Writings of Benjamin Franklin*. Ed. Albert Henry Smyth. New York: Macmillan, 1905.

Franklin, Benjamin, William Temple Franklin, and William Duane. *Memoirs of Benjamin Franklin*. Philadelphia: M'Carty & Davis, 1834.

Frey, Sylvia R. *Water from the Rock: Black Resistance in a Revolutionary Age*. Princeton, NJ: Princeton University Press, 1991.

Frohnen, Bruce, ed. *The Anti-Federalists: Selected Writings and Speeches*. Washington, DC: Regnery Pub., 1999.

George III (King of Great Britain). *The Correspondence of King George the Third with Lord North from 1768 to 1783*. London: John Murray, 1867.

Gordon, John Steele. *An Empire of Wealth: The Epic History of American Economic Power*. New York: Harper Perennial, 2005.

"Government Spending Chart in United States." *Government Spending in United States*. Ed. Christopher Chantrill. 09 May 2011. <www.usgovernmentspending.com/charts.html>.

Grossman, Richard S. *Unsettled Account: The Evolution of Banking in the Industrialized World since 1800*. Princeton, N.J.: Princeton University Press, 2010.

Hamilton, Alexander. *The Papers of Alexander Hamilton*. Ed. Harold C. Syrett and Jacob E. Cooke. New York: Columbia University Press, 1961.

Hamilton, Alexander. *The Works of Alexander Hamilton*. Ed. Henry Cabot Lodge. New York: G.P. Putnam's Sons, 1904.

Hamilton, Alexander. *The Works of Alexander Hamilton*. Ed. John C. Hamilton. New York: John F. Trow, 1850.

Hamilton, Alexander, John Jay, and James Madison. *The Federalist Papers*. New York: J. and M. Lean, 1788. The Constitution Society. <www.constitution.org/fed/federa00.htm>.

Hamilton, James A. *Reminiscences of James A. Hamilton; Or, Men and Events, at Home and Abroad, during Three Quarters of a Century*. New York: C. Scribner &, 1869.

Henry, William Wirt. *Patrick Henry; Life, Correspondence and Speeches*. New York: Charles Scribner's Sons, 1891.

Hitchens, Christopher. "Cruiser." Foreword. *First in Peace: How George Washington Set the Course for America*. By Conor Cruise O'Brien. Cambridge, MA: Da Capo, 2009. 1-16.

Howe, William. *The Narrative of Lieut. Gen. Sir William Howe*. London: H. Baldwin, 1780.

Hudelson, Richard. *Modern Political Philosophy*. Armonk, NY: M.E. Sharpe, 1999.

Isaacson, Walter. *Benjamin Franklin: An American Life*. New York: Simon & Schuster, 2003.

Jay, John. *The Correspondence and Public Papers of John Jay*. Ed. Henry Phelps Johnston. New York: G.P. Putnam's Sons, 1890.

Jefferson, Thomas. *The Writings of Thomas Jefferson*. Ed. H. A. Washington. Washington: Taylor & Maury, 1853-59.

Jefferson, Thomas. *The Writings of Thomas Jefferson*. Ed. Paul Leicester Ford. New York: G.P. Putnam's Sons, 1892-99.

Johnson, Paul. *A History of the American People*. New York: HarperCollins, 1997.

Knox, John Jay. *A History of Banking in the United States*. Ed. Bradford Rhodes and Elmer H. Youngman. New York: Bradford Rhodes, 1900.

Lane, Carl. "For "A Positive Profit": The Federal Investment in the First Bank of the United States, 1792-1802." *The William and Mary Quarterly* 54 (July 1997): 601-12.

Lutz, Donald. *A Preface to American Political Theory*. Lawrence: Kansas University Press, 1992.

MacDonald, William, ed. *Documentary Source Book of American History, 1606-1898*. New York: Macmillan, 1908.

Mackesy, Piers. *The War for America: 1775-1783*. Lincoln: University of Nebraska, 1992.

Madison, James. *The Debates in the Federal Convention of 1787: Which Framed the Constitution of the United States of America*. Ed. Gaillard Hunt and James Brown Scott. Amherst, NY: Prometheus, 2007.

Madison, James. *Letters and Other Writings of James Madison*. Philadelphia: J. B. Lippincott, 1965.

Madison, James. *The Writings of James Madison*. Ed. Gaillard Hunt. New York: G.P. Putnam's Sons, 1910.

Maier, Pauline. *American Scripture: Making the Declaration of Independence*. New York: Alfred A. Knopf, 1997.

Marshall, John. *The Life of George Washington*. Philadelphia: C.P. Wayne, 1807.

Mason, George. "Virginia Declaration of Rights." *Avalon Project*. Yale Law School Lillian Goldman Law Library, 2008. <avalon.law.yale.edu/18th_century/virginia.asp>.

McClellan, James. *Liberty, Order, and Justice*. Third ed. Indianapolis: Liberty Fund, 2000.

McClelland, Peter D. "The Cost to America of British Imperial Policy." *The American Economic Review*. Vol. 59. No. 2 (May 1969): 370-81.

McCullough, David. "What the Fog Wrought." *What If?: The World's Foremost Military Historians Imagine What Might Have Been*. Ed. Robert Cowley. New York: Berkley, 2000. 189-200.

McMaster, John Bach, and Frederick Dawson Stone. *Pennsylvania and the Federal Constitution, 1787-1788*. Lancaster, PA: Inquirer Printing and Pub., 1888.

Meese, Edwin. *The Heritage Guide to the Constitution*. Washington, D.C.: Heritage Foundation, 2005.

Meyerson, Michael I. *Liberty's Blueprint: How Madison and Hamilton Wrote the Federalist Papers, Defined the Constitution, and Made Democracy Safe for the World*. New York: Basic Books, 2008.

Middleton, Richard. *Colonial America: A History, 1565 - 1776*. Third ed. Malden, Mass: Blackwell, 2007.

Montesquieu, Charles De Secondat. *Considerations on the Causes of the Greatness of the Romans and Their Decline*. Trans. David Lowenthal. New York: Free, 1965.

Montesquieu, Charles De Secondat. *The Spirit of Laws*. Trans. Thomas Nugent. London: J. Nourse and P. Vaillant, 1766.

Nash, Gary B. *The Forgotten Fifth: African Americans in the Age of Revolution*. Cambridge, MA: Harvard University Press, 2006.

Nettels, Curtis P. *The Emergence of a National Economy: 1775-1815*. Armonk, NY: M. E. Sharpe, 1989.

Niles, Hezekiah. *Centennial Offering. Republication of the Principles and Acts of the Revolution in America*. New York: A. S. Barnes, 1876.

O'Brien, Conor Cruise. *First in Peace: How George Washington Set the Course for America*. Cambridge, MA: Da Capo, 2009.

Osberg, Lars, and Fazley Siddiq. "The Inequality Of Wealth in Britain's North American Colonies: The Importance Of The Relatively Poor." *Review of Income and Wealth* 34.2 (1988): 143-63.

Paine, Thomas, Sidney Hook, and Jack Fruchtman. *Common Sense, Rights of Man, and Other Essential Writings of Thomas Paine*. New York: Signet Classic, 2003.

Perlmutter, Philip. *The Dynamics of American Ethnic, Religious, and Racial Group Life: An Interdisciplinary Overview*. Westport, CT: Praeger, 1996.

Phillips, Kevin. *The Cousins' Wars: Religion, Politics, and the Triumph of Anglo-America*. New York, NY: Basic Books, 1999.

Pitt, William, Edmund Burke, and Thomas Erskine. *Celebrated Speeches of Chatham, Burke, and Erskine*. Philadelphia: E.C. & J. Biddle, 1840.

Polybius. *The Histories*. Trans. W. R. Paton. *Loeb Classical Library*. Harvard University Press, 1922 thru 1927.

Pellew, George. *American Statesmen: John Jay*. Boston: Houghton, Mifflin and Company, 1890.

Plato. *Republic*. Trans. Paul Shorey. *Plato in Twelve Volumes*. Cambridge, MA: Harvard University Press, 1969.

Platt, Suzy, ed. *Respectfully Quoted: a Dictionary of Quotations*. New York: Barnes & Noble, 1993.

Quarles, Benjamin. *The Negro in the American Revolution*. Chapel Hill: University of North Carolina, 1996.

Raphael, Ray. *A People's History of the American Revolution: How Common People Shaped the Fight for Independence*. New York: New, 2001.

Raphael, Ray. *Founding Myths: Stories That Hide Our Patriotic Past*. New York: New Press, 2004.

"Ratification Dates and Votes." *The U.S. Constitution Online*. USConstitution.net. 24 Jan. 2011. <www.usconstitution.net/ratifications.html>.

Reed, William B. *Life and Correspondence of Joseph Reed*. Philadelphia: Lindsay and Blakiston, 1847.

Roosevelt, Theodore. *New York*. New York: Longmans, Green, and Co., 1891.

Schweikart, Larry. *The Entrepreneurial Adventure: A History of Business in the United States*. Fort Worth: Harcourt College, 2000.

Shepherd, James F. "British America and the Atlantic Economy." *The Economy of Early America: The Revolutionary Period, 1763-1790*. Ed. Ronald Hoffman. Charlottesville: University of Virginia, 1988. 3-44.

Shy, John W. *A People Numerous and Armed: Reflections on the Military Struggle for American Independence*. Revised ed. Ann Arbor: University of Michigan, 1990.

Skousen, W. Cleon. *The 5000 Year Leap: A Miracle That Changed the World*. National Center for Constitutional Studies, 2009.

Smith, Adam. *An Inquiry into the Nature and Causes of the Wealth of Nations*. Ed. Edwin Cannan. New York: Modern Library, 1994.

Sobran, Joseph. "Foreword." *The Anti-Federalists: Selected Writings and Speeches*. Ed. Bruce Frohnen. Washington, DC: Regnery Pub., 1999. Vii-Xi.

Sparks, Jared. *The Life of Gouverneur Morris: With Selections from His Correspondence and Miscellaneous Papers*. Boston: Gray & Bowen, 1832.

Stauber, Leland G. *The American Revolution: A Grand Mistake*. Amherst, NY: Prometheus, 2010.

Swett, Samuel. *History of Bunker Hill Battle: With a Plan*. Boston: Munroe and Francis, 1826.

"The Declaration of Rights of the Stamp Act Congress, October 19, 1765." *Constitution Society*. <www.constitution.org/bcp/dor_sac.htm>.

Thomas, Robert Paul. "A Quantitative Approach to the Study of the Effects of British Imperial Policy upon Colonial Welfare: Some Preliminary Findings." *The Journal of Economic History*. Vol. 25. No. 4 (Dec 1965): 615-38.

Tiedemann, Joseph S. "Patriots by Default: Queens County, New York, and the British Army, 1776-1783." *The William and Mary Quarterly*, Third Series, Vol. 43, No. 1 (January 1986): 35-63.

Tocqueville, Alexis de. *Democracy in America and Two Essays on America*. Trans. Gerald E. Bevan. London: Penguin, 2003.

"United States Federal State and Local Government Spending." *Government Spending in the United States of America*. Ed. Christopher Chantrill. <www.usgovernment spending.com>.

Wallis, John Joseph. "Sovereign Default and Repudiation: The Emerging-Market Debt Crisis in U.S. States, 1839-1843." (2004).

Ward, A. W., G. W. Prothero, and Stanley Leathes. *The Cambridge Modern History*. New York: Macmillan Co., 1903.

Washington, George. *The Writings of George Washington*. Ed. John C. Fitzpatrick. Washington: United States Printing Office, 1931-44.

Washington, George. *The Writings of George Washington*. Ed. Jared Sparks. Boston: Russell, Odiorne, and Metcalf, 1833-37.

"Washington and the Constitution." *The Literary World* 20.7 (March 1889): 105-106.

Watson, John F. *Annals of Philadelphia and Pennsylvania, in the Olden Time*. Philadelphia: John Penington and Uriah Hunt, 1844.

Webster, Daniel. *Newly Discovered Fourth of July Oration*. Boston: A. Williams, 1882.

Wells, William. *Life and Public Services of Samuel Adams*. Boston: Little, Brown and, 1865.

Whately, Thomas. *The Regulations Lately Made concerning the Colonies and the Taxes Imposed upon Them Considered*. London: Printed for J. Wilkie, 1765.

Wilson, James. "Speech of October 6, 1787." Philadelphia. *Constitution Society*. <www.constitution.org/afp/jwilson0.htm>.

Wilson, James. *The Works of James Wilson*. Ed. James DeWitt Andrews. Vol. 1. Callaghan and, 1895.

Wood, Gordon S. *The American Revolution: A History*. New York: Modern Library, 2002.

INDEX

L

M

N

CPSIA information can be obtained at www.ICGtesting.com
Printed in the USA
BVOW021646290911

272312BV00003B/79/P